The Palaces and Parks in Pushkin

LIUDMILA LAPINA

The Palaces and Parks in PUSHKIN

A Guide

RADUGA PUBLISHERS
MOSCOW

ДВОРЦЫ-МУЗЕИ И ПАРКИ ПУШКИНА
Путеводитель
На английском языке
Редакция литературы по спорту и туризму

Translated from the Russian by *Glenys Ann Rampley*
Editor of the Russian text *Marta Derzhavina*
Editor of the English text *Alexander Kafyrov*
Designed by *Vladimir Miroshnichenko*
Art editor *Alexandra Tomchinskaya*
Layout by *Elena Cherepova*
Photos by *Boris Stezhko*
Maps by *Lyubov Cheltsova*

Л $\dfrac{1905040100-100}{031\,(05)-86}$ 061−85

ISBN 5-05-000071-8

CONTENTS

PLACES CONNECTED WITH ALEXANDER PUSHKIN

THE CATHERINE PALACE. THE PARKS

ABOUT THIS BOOK

The town of Pushkin is one of the many gems of Russian art, unique in its fortunate combination of outstanding architecture and splendid parks. Here you can visit places connected with the life and works of the great Russian poet Alexander Pushkin. The palaces in Pushkin are a real encyclopaedia of the best creations by the outstanding masters of the eighteenth and ninteenth centuries, brought together into a magnificent complex.

Our guidebook invites you to visit the places associated with Pushkin, the palaces and the monuments in the parks, and see for yourself the beautiful things of the past preserved and restored.

WHERE IT IS

The town of Pushkin is 24 km from Leningrad in the Izhorsk heights, which rise to 150–170 m above sea level. The landscape here varies greatly, just as if nature had intended it to be made into parks. Hills, stony ridges, and terraces alternate with valleys, horizontal and sloping plains; woodland gives way to fields. The numerous springs are the sources of streams and feed the ponds and pools.

Pushkin has a special microclimate as it is situated fairly high above sea level. The influence of the Gulf of Finland and the Atlantic is felt less here than in other places in the Leningrad region so that the annual precipitation brought by the air masses from the sea is less, and there are more sunny, cloudless days. The warmest month is July and the coldest January, but the average annual temperature in the Pushkin region is plus 4.5 °C. The microclimate is also affected by the luxuriant greenery in which the town is literally bathed, causing the breezes to be gentle and the daily and yearly temperature range to be smaller.

PAGES OF HISTORY

The land of Izhora* where the town of Pushkin with its world famous monuments is now situated has a many-century-long history. Its territory, which lies to the south of the Gulf of Finland and the river Neva had long formed part of the ancient Russian state and was closely linked with the most important stages in the emergence of Ancient Rus. From the twelfth century this area was referred to in the chronicles as the Izhora Lands of the "Lord of Great Novgorod", as the independent feudal state focussed on Novgorod in north-western Rus was called at that time. In the twelfth to fifteenth centuries the centre of the Izhora lands was the town of Oreshek situated at the source of the Neva flowing from Lake Ladoga. Thick forests and swamps surrounded the sparsely scattered villages. This territory was vital to the Novgorod feudal republic since the main trade route linking Novgorod with western countries lay along the Neva and the Gulf of Finland at that time.

* The Izhora lands or Izhora was the name given to the territory situated on the banks of the Neva and to the south-west of Lake Ladoga in the twelfth to eighteenth centuries. These parts were inhabited by the Izhors, a small people speaking a language of the Finno-Ugrian group.—*Ed.*

The people of Novgorod strove to become firmly established here, to bar the way into the Russian lands to the Swedes and the German feudal lords, to safeguard their trade routes to countries overseas. Therefore, from the twelfth century onwards the left bank of the Neva became the scene of bitter fighting. In the second half of the fifteenth century all the Russian lands united around Moscow, and Great Novgorod also became part of the Moscow principality.

The state of Moscow was, however, undermined by its defeat in the Livonian war (1558-1583), which the Russian tsar Ivan IV waged against the Livonian Order, Sweden, Poland and the Great Principality of Lithuania to obtain an outlet to the Baltic Sea, and also by the struggle among the boyar groupings for power after the death of Ivan IV. Taking advantage of this situation, the Swedes occupied the Izhora lands. It was not until 1702 during the Great Northern War (1700-1721) between Russia and Sweden that Russian forces took Oreshek by storm. The first reference to this locality where Tsarskoye Selo, now the town of Pushkin, was subsequently to spring up, dates back to that year.

To begin with, there were the dilapidated wooden structures of a small estate called Saari muis in Finnish, which means "farm on an elevated spot". This farm, which is mentioned in the documents and maps of the end of the seventeenth and the beginning of the eighteenth century, consisted of a mansion, (the owner's house), service premises, stables, a farm and poultry yards, a carriage shed, a barn, and a modest garden divided into four square plots of land by two perpendicular paths. The mansion and service premises crowned the ridge, which sloped down to the little river Vangasi.

During the Great Northern War Peter the Great had already been making gifts of the lands near the new capital, St. Petersburg (founded in 1703), to his retainers for the latter to develop them. The Saari farm was first presented to the governor-general of the liberated area, Alexander Menshikov, and then on May 30, 1710, on the instructions of Peter the Great, it was "bequeathed" to the tsar's wife, the future empress Catherine I. Peasants from other parts of Russia were brought there by force, and two hundred peasant homes, a brick and tile works and farm buildings appeared here.

In 1717, when the city of St. Petersburg, which was completely unlike any of the old Russian towns, mushroomed rapidly on the banks of the Neva, the first stone buildings were erected for the tsar in Saari muis. Designed by the architect Johann Braunstein, the two-storey stone edifice erected by 1723, was of strikingly simple and modest appearance, with the unpretentious jambs and lintels of its doors and windows and a gambrel roof. Simplicity, as well as the functionality of the building's design were characteristic features of the architecture in the first quarter of the eighteenth century.

While the palace was being erected in Saari muis, work was begun on laying out a French (Dutch) garden with the help of Jan Roozen, who had planned the

Summer Gardens in St. Petersburg. In 1718, tens of thousands of maples, limes, elms, birches, poplars, fruit trees, and decorative shrubs were brought here. The gentle slope in front of the palace was transformed into descending terraces, connected by steps. The garden was laid out on these terraces. The upper part of the garden, adjacent to the palace, came to be known as the Upper Garden, and the part lower down as the Lower Park. Along the Vangasi River, which flowed along the bottom of a ravine, a large hexagonal pond was constructed. A mill was worked by the water flowing out of the pond. At that time summer-houses, hotbeds, and conservatories were set up in the garden. A Vast tract of natural woodland to the north-west of the palace was fenced off and turned into a Menagerie where elk, wild boars, and hares were kept for the tsar's hunt. Another pond was made in the northern part of the Menagerie by damming the river Kuzminka. This is what the tsar's new estate, which came to be known soon after as Tsarskoye Selo (the Tsar's Village) looked like in the 1720s.

Subsequently, the Upper and Lower Gardens were incorporated into the Catherine Park and the Menagerie part into the Alexander Park, but they have retained their names to this day.

The most impressive stage in the construction of the park and palace in Tsarskoye Selo dates back to the reign of Peter the Great's daughter Elizabeth (1741-1761), or to be more exact, to 1740s-1750s. On the site of the modest palace of Catherine I, a luxurious summer residence was created for Elizabeth, striking in its magnificence and splendour with its huge gardens and variety of decorative structures.

The compositional centre of the tsar's residence was the palace, the reconstruction of which was begun in 1742 by Mikhail Zemtsov, an outstanding architect, who had designed the monumental Anichkov Palace in St. Petersburg, and was continued by his pupils Andrei Kvasov and Savva Chevakinsky. The architects retained the old Catherine Palace, enclosing its walls and foundations in the main body of the palace as the "Central House". Four rectangular pavilions were built onto its corners, making symmetrical avant-corps in the form of three windows along the façade. The Great (Upper) Hall of the Catherine Palace was subjected to alterations: the architects made the hall higher and longer, adding an upper mezzanine floor and a row of windows and completely changed the shape of the roof.

The larger dimensions of the main building allowed another two big rooms to be created on the upper storey and a main staircase to be built to the first floor. The façades of the "Central House" were embellished anew with pilasters and a figured pediment. In the autumn of 1744 the builders completed two new wings of the palace complex. According to Kvasov's design, they were connected with the "Central House" by single-storey wooden galleries, colonnades, which were rebuilt in stone a year later by Chevakinsky.

In 1745, the buildings around the palace were completed and brought under one roof, these single-storey domestic wings forming a colossal arc girding the main courtyard. These semicircular buildings emphasized the huge dimensions of the palace and determined the configuration of the square on the western façade. So, this splendid palace amidst its parks stood on the crest of the hill, dominating the surrounding countryside.

In the following years Chevakinsky became the principal architect involved in "the great reconstruction at Tsarskoye Selo". He designed the five-domed stone Church of the Resurrection with a bell-tower to stand near the right wing and he reconstructed the conservatory hall, which became the Portrait Gallery. According to Chevakinsky's plans, the palace ensemble was united into a single whole by hanging gardens. When these structures had been completed in 1746, the enormous palace became 306 metres long.

Work on the exteriors and interiors of the rooms in the palace and of the new buildings in the ensemble continued from 1746 to 1751. Skilful craftsmen and thousands of serfs embellished the façades with ornaments, gilt statues and moulded decorations, and the interiors with plaster and carving. However, in May 1752, when all the decorations were finished and the façades of the palace glistened with gold, the Empress Elizabeth thought that the palace did not look sufficiently luxurious and elegant for large receptions and festivities. Reconstruction of the Tsarskoye Selo ensemble began, and even the finished parts of the buildings were demolished. The architect Bartholomeo Rastrelli was commissioned to make fresh alterations to the palace. By that time this outstanding master of Russian baroque architecture was already famous for the splendid edifices he had erected in St. Petersburg and Kiev.

The baroque style was in its heyday in the 1740s and 1750s in palace building in Russia, which had become a mighty world power, and, to quote Mikhail Lomonosov, the Russian scholar of encyclopaedic knowledge, a poet and artist, which needed "its own splendour in its decorous majesty". The solemnity, magnificence, and scale characteristic of baroque art corresponded to the firmly established national awareness of the Russians, who had confidently entered the world arena; it best corresponded to the striving in Russia at that time to appear imposing and extoll the power of the emperor, to assert Russia's place as a state of feudal lords and gentry once and for all.

The buildings of huge dimensions and extraordinarily luxurious, elegant façades did, as it were, embody the might of the Russian state in monuments of architecture. This was precisely the reason why the art forms of baroque which had taken shape in the West and been transferred to Russian soil, acquired profoundly unique national features there.

Rastrelli made extensive use of the traditions of old Russian architecture in his buildings and also of the experience gained by architects at the time of Peter the Great. The edifices in Tsarskoye Selo have a place of honour among his numerous buildings and are distinguished for the tremendous plasticity of their architectural forms, the brightness of the colours and the splendour of their ornamentation.

In four years (the main reconstruction of the palace took from 1752 to 1756 to complete), preserving the basic principles of the ensemble's existing layout, Rastrelli created a country mansion, in accordance with the demands of the tsar's court. The building was so magnificent and splendid that it literally dazzled his contemporaries with the inexhaustible fantasy in its elaborate decoration.

When making the new alterations, Rastrelli raised the single-storey galleries to the height of the side wings, and erected a third floor on the Central House, thereby turning the central part of the building into a single continuous massif of tremendous length. Above the gallery leading to the left wing, the architect designed a vast hall with two rows of windows and glass doors.

Rastrelli left an open gallery between the right wing and the church, having arranged a hanging garden there and enclosing it in walls at the sides for symmetry's sake. He raised the cupola and domes of the church high above the façades of the palace and erected a cupola with a spire above the portrait gallery. He moved the main staircase to the southern part of the building. Now anyone coming into the main courtyard through the new northern open-work wrought-iron gates made to Rastrelli's design at the Sestroretsk Works (an armoury, now an instrument-making factory in the town of Sestroretsk near Leningrad), could

Main façade of Catherine Palace.

not fail to notice the façades of the tsar's residence and admire its splendour, before he entered it. The palace did indeed give the impression of extraordinary festiveness and elegance. The architect's striving for splendour and refinement is evident in the play of light and shade caused by the picturesque break in the line of the façade and in the rhythmic system of the numerous columns and pilasters, the luxurious window casings, the glittering gilding of the sculptured decoration, the moulded and carved ornamentation, and the azure colour of the walls.

Sculptures predominate in the decoration on the façades. Powerful figures of Atlas (sculptor Johann Dunker) with their heads bent low as if weighed down by an enormous burden, support the columns of the upper storey. These figures and also the large, boldly and dynamically moulded male masks mounted on the piers are among the most significant ornaments on the palace façades even now. The impression was enhanced by the gilded wooden sculptures and vases on the balustrade along the roof which have not survived to our day.

People at that time were carried away by the luxuriousness of the rooms in the palace, their varied artistic decor, the expressiveness of the carved forms, the bright colours, the rich play of light and shade, the abundance of gilded carved patterns running along the walls. Not only the walls but also the doors connecting the halls were lavishly decorated with intricate gilded carving and produced the impression that you were walking down a golden corridor. It is not accidental that the main suite was called the Golden Suite at that time.

The walls, doors and corners of the windows of the antechambers, five rooms for people waiting to attend official receptions, were also richly decorated with gilded carving. The carved ornamentation in the first and second antechambers appears to spurt upwards along the tall, narrow pilasters, covering the cornices with gold ornaments and twisting into the volutes and scrolls of the sconces and brackets of the candlesticks.

The extraordinary splendour of the palace's Great Hall abounding in gilded carving, is quite breathtaking. This carving frames the mirrors and windows either in the shape of rich full figures and volutes or a thin, almost flat ornament covered with gold leaf.

Some 100 kilogrammes of gold were used on the ornamentation of the palace, from which goldsmiths forged leaf thinner than cigarette paper.

The residence in Tsarskoye Selo was created by the labour of folk craftsmen, thousands of working people. Skilled workmen and stonemasons, painters and sculptors were brought there from all corners of Russia. Numerous soldiers and sailors were also engaged on the construction work. Living in extremely difficult conditions in tents and dug-outs and working 12 to 14 hours a day "from morn till night", they drained the land, cleared the woodland thickets, dug ponds and canals, and built roads. The artistic items needed for Tsarskoye Selo were made by the Sestroretsk and Tula armouries, stone cutting works in the Urals, and numerous private enterprises.

To impart the necessary splendour to the Tsarskoye Selo ensemble, its principal architects, Chevakinsky and Rastrelli, had to tackle the highly involved tasks of reconstructing the parks, gardens and building numerous pavilions and summer-houses.

The gardens were of the so called French type which were common in Europe at that time. Geometrical shapes predominated in their planning and they were kept strictly symmetrical. Trees clipped in the shape of figures were planted in rows lining long straight avenues intended for the courtiers' promenades. Many of the decorative trees and shrubs were transplanted to the parks in Tsarskoye Selo from the gardens in St. Petersburg, and some such as yew-trees, box-trees and others were obtained from abroad.

The whimsical shapes of the bushes and trees echoed the architecture of the small structures. The marble statues brought to Tsarskoye Selo from St. Petersburg blended organically into the composition of the park. Peter the Great commissioned these sculptures from well-known masters of the Venetian school such as Pietro Baratta, Giovanni Bonazza, Antonio Tarsia, and Giovanni Zarzoni; the glory and might of the Russian empire was to be expressed allegorically in personages from ancient mythology.

The numerous ponds and canals with picturesque winding sides and banks were a traditional feature of symmetrical parks; during the reconstruction of the park, therefore, the Vittolovsky Canal was laid and a 16-kilometre-long gravity-flow pipeline dug from the springs in the village of Taitsa to the park's artificial ponds and lakes. One of the main water bodies in the Old Garden, the Great Pond, was fed by the Vittolovsky Canal, along the banks of which the Grotto and Slide pavilions, popular entertainments at that time, were situated. These pavilions designed by Rastrelli, their façades embellished with moulded ornaments, the wrought-iron grilles of the doors and their high roofs, decorated with gilded carving, were picturesquely reflected in the quiet waters of the pond. At this time, the Hermitage, a small but very luxuriously decorated amusement pavilion, was completed. Another amusement pavilion, "Mon Bijou" was created by Rastrelli in the middle of the Menagerie, i.e. on the other side of the palace.

By the end of 1756, the residence at Tsarskoye Selo with its huge gardens and wide variety of decorative structures was completed and assumed an appearance typical of Russian baroque architecture. Henceforth, official receptions for the Russian nobility and foreign ambassadors were held at Tsarskoye Selo.

The next stage in the construction of Tsarskoye Selo dates back to the 1770s. At that time, in Russia, as in many other countries of Europe, there was a tendency for the strict "classical" forms of architecture of Ancient Greece and Rome to be revived. This trend was engendered on the eve of the French Revolution, in an atmosphere of the political struggle of the young and progressive bourgeoisie of that time against the moribund feudal world and was a reflection of its ideology. These progressive aesthetic strivings of the epoch, the new ideas on beauty in art connected with the development of rationalist philosophy, with the attainments of the precise sciences, took shape in Russia in the mid-eighteenth century under the influence of the representatives of the Enlightenment such as Mikhail Lomonosov, Nikolai Novikov, and Alexander Sumarokov. These scholars considered the glorification of one's homeland and the instilling of patriotic feelings in their fellow citizens to be the greatest purpose of art. Turning to the history of the people and national problems in their works, they believed that Russia could only effect social changes and overcome benightedness and the lack of rights of the people via enlightenment.

The architects of Russia who were closely connected with national traditions, interpreted classical forms in their own way, creating an original style known as Russian classicism. The profoundly national character of the new style determined its progressive role and imparted extraordinary force and maturity to the whole of Russian art in the second half of the eighteenth century.

In contradistinction to the luxurious express baroque structures, buildings in the classical style were characterised by a preciseness of architectural forms, an accuracy of proportions, the predominance of strict, straight lines and the majestic solemnity of the exterior. The façades of the buildings of the classical period which were harmonious in all their details, were usually arranged in three parts. The centre of the edifice was distinguished by the portico sandwiched between symmetrical wings, more modest in design, with little ornamentation. Drawing on the art of antiquity, Russian architecture at that time applied classical examples in a free manner, reinterpreting them in accordance with the national background and traditions.

The formation of the palace ensemble in Tsarskoye Selo in the 1770s also bears witness to the complicated process of the gradual change-over from magnificence and refined splendour to a more austere style, more harmonious proportions, and the simplicity of the structures characteristic of classicism.

Just as in the 1750s fabulous sums of money and tremendous effort were expended on the development and decoration of Tsarskoye Selo. It was the favourite residence of the Empress Catherine the Great (1762-1796), who, in accordance with the shift in artistic tastes at the end of the 1770s and the beginning of the 1780s, when the magnificence of Rastrelli's architecture began to be regarded as barbarous luxury, wished to have buildings in the new style in Tsarskoye Selo.

The classical canons are reflected in the structures erected in Tsarskoye Selo by the architects Vasili Neyelov and his sons, Ilya Neyelov and Peter Neyelov, who devoted the whole of their creative lives to the construction of the palaces and gardens in Tsarskoye Selo. Their names are connected in particular with the laying out of the natural park. This type of park became popular in Russia when it was fashionable to make parks and gardens look natural. Therefore the trees and shrubs in the Catherine Park were no longer clipped and soon became so overgrown that they hid the pavilions. The park was extended considerably. A new landscaped park was created by the gardeners Johann Busch and Trifon Ilyin, planned by Vasili Neyelov, to the south-west of the Old Garden, around the Great Pond and to the west of it. The winding paths and different shaped glades, the weeping willows and birches dotted about on the edges of the ponds and lakes, the numerous summer houses, pavilions, and little bridges which appeared to be scattered about in the most unexpected nooks, all contrasted sharply with the emphatically arranged symmetrical part of the park.

The park ensemble that took shape in Tsarskoye Selo in the 1770s was one of the major landscape parks in Russia.

Besides the classical buildings, Vasili Neyelov erected several decorative structures in Tsarskoye Selo in the Chinese style popular at that time, a combination of classical features and the whimsical forms of Chinese architecture. The most typical of these structures is the so-called "Grande Caprice", a massive archway set up at the entrance to the Tsarskoye Selo estate on the old St. Petersburg road, now the boundary of the Catherine and Alexander parks. The heavy archway faced with rough stone is crowned with a light, tracery summer house. Eight columns of pink marble support the octagonal roof of the summer house with its edges curving upwards and its intricate ornament. The Petite Caprice bridge was finished in Chinese style by Vasili Neyelov and a court theatre, which came to be known as the Chinese Theatre, was designed by Ilya Neyelov.

At the same time as the park pavilions were being built, on the orders of the Catherine the Great, fresh alterations were made to the Great Palace, which she thought was not roomy enough, under the supervision of Vasili Neyelov. In 1775, two symmetrical stone buildings of extremely plain exterior designed by him were erected around the circumference. A few years later, in 1779-1784, his son Ilya Neyelov erected a separate wing of the palace to the north of the main building but connected with it by a monumental arch across the road. The plainess and austere design of the building, which later became the Tsarskoye Selo Lyceum (to be described later in the book) contrasted with the magnificence of Rastrelli's palace.

In the 1780s two outstanding architects of that time, Charles Cameron and Giacomo Quarenghi were commissioned to take charge of the most important construction work in Tsarskoye Selo. These passionate admirers of ancient Greek and Roman art, seeing in the strict lines and fine proportions of ancient architecture an inexhaustible source of beauty and inspiration, created a number of magnificent classical structures in Tsarskoye Selo, thereby entering brilliant pages in the history of Russian architecture.

In 1780-1795, Charles Cameron designed a complex of structures on an antique subject — the Cold Bath, or the Agate Rooms and the Ramp. At the same time, Cameron worked on finishing the newly built premises in the palace, including a main staircase. Cameron's palace interiors are distinguished for the beauty and grandeur of their proportions, and the strictness of their decoration, in which the architect creatively employs the principles of antique art.

Interesting monuments of Russian classical architecture, distinguished by austere simplicity of forms and restraint of artistic principles were created in Tsarskoye Selo by the Italian Giacomo Quarenghi, one of the outstanding architects of the end of the eighteenth and beginning of the nineteenth centuries to whom Russia became a second homeland.

Giacomo Quarenghi designed many large edifices in St. Petersburg, such as the Academy of Sciences, the Smolny Institute, and others. In Pushkin today the park pavilions, the Concert Hall, the Ruined Kitchen, the Hall on the island of the Great Pond erected in the 1780s are reminiscent of Quarenghi's early works.

In 1792-1795, Quarenghi built a palace in Tsarskoye Selo for the grandson of Catherine the Great, Alexander (the future tsar Alexander I). In its dimensions this building was the largest to appear in Tsarskoye Selo in the second half of the eighteenth century. Just as the magnificent Catherine Palace is characteristic of the architecture of the mid-eighteenth century, so is the Alexander Palace with its magnificent Corinthian colonnade accentuating the compositional centre, with its austere façades almost devoid of decoration, typical of its own time.

Monuments of military glory dedicated to the victories of the Russian forces in the war with Turkey in 1768–1774 were created by the architect A. Rinaldi in the style of early classicism. These are: the Cheshme Column, the Kagul Obelisk, the Morea (or Small Rostral) Column, and others, which blend splendidly into the landscape of the park, a perfect imitation of nature untouched.

The shaping of the architectural appearance of Tsarskoye Selo in the first half of the nineteenth century is connected with the name of the remarkable architect Vasili Stasov, a representative of late Russian classicism. The interiors of the Blue Drawing-Room created by him, the personal apartments of Alexander I, and the bed-chamber of his mother Mariya Fyodorovna are distinguished by the simplicity of forms characteristic of this architectural trend in Russia. The wing of the palace erected by Ilya Neyelov in 1789–1791 was redesigned by Stasov to house the Lyceum, an educational establishment for the privileged children of courtiers of exalted rank.

Among the architects of Tsarskoye

Tsarskoye Selo, water colour by an unknown artist, early 19th century.

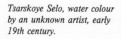

Selo in this period mention should be made of the Italian architect Luigi Rusca, who designed the Granite Terrace at the top of the slope to the Great Pond and completed the pavilion known as the "Evening Hall".

In the 1850s, the architect Ippolito Monighetti built a Turkish bath on the edge of the Great Pond. This was a decorative structure reminiscent of a mosque with its tall minaret, delicate mosaic decorations and gilded cupola.

In the second half of the nineteenth century no buildings of great artistic value were added to the Tsarskoye Selo ensemble, and no significant changes were made in the planning and boundaries of the Catherine Park. The only exception here was the monument to Alexander Pushkin by the sculptor Rudolf Bach unveiled in 1900 in the little garden of the Lyceum.

After the October Socialist Revolution, the palaces and parks in Tsarskoye Selo were taken under the protection of the state and were proclaimed the property of the people by government decree. By the end of 1917, on the initiative of Lenin, a commission for museums and the conservation of monuments of art treasures of olden times had already been set up under the People's Commissariat of Education. At that time, although there was Civil War in Russia, causing economic dislocation, the Soviet of People's Commissars found it possible to allot means for repairs and restoration work on the palaces formerly belonging to the royal family.

In 1923, the well-known art historian and artist Alexander Benois wrote: "We were all witnesses to the astounding phenomenon that the most critical moments of the Russian Revolution occurred without hardly any harm being done to historical and artistic monuments... Once again we were able to visit Tsarskoye, Pavlovsk, Gatchina, Oranienbaum, and Peterhof* and admire all their beauty just as if nothing had happened, acknowledging that the best and most interesting aspects of what had disappeared remained imprinted for us and for future generations."

After the revolution numerous children's sanatoria and holiday camps were housed in the former high society residences and summer cottages of Tsarskoye Selo, and in 1918 the town was renamed Detskoye Selo (Children's Village). Since 1937 it has been called Pushkin, to perpetuate the memory of the great Russian poet, Alexander Pushkin, who spent his youth there.

On June 9, 1918, the opening ceremony of the history and art museum in the palace at Tsarskoye Selo took place. For the first time in two centuries the doors of the former tsars' residence were opened wide to the people at large. Right from the early years of Soviet government the fine collections here provided aids with which to educate the common people, and these palaces, now museums,

---

* The environs of Leningrad (at that time Petrograd), which are, like Pushkin, famous for their parks and palaces.—*Ed.*

became genuine centres of culture, where the working people could be educated in aesthetics. The parks and palaces in Pushkin became more and more popular with every passing year.

The Second World War interrupted the peaceful existence of Soviet people. Pushkin was under Nazi occupation for more than two years. Units of Hitler's army were billeted in the palaces, stocks of ammunition, and forges and garages were housed there, and weapon emplacements were set up in the park pavilions. Although the most valuable exhibits in the museum—the paintings, furniture, articles of applied art—had been evacuated to the depths of the country by governmental decree and the marble and bronze sculptures safely buried in the ground, the occupying forces managed to do tremendous, at times irreparable damage, to the ensembles in Pushkin. The halls of the palace and the park pavilions were destroyed by fire. The amber panels from the famous Amber Room were removed and taken away, as well as the painted plafonds, and valuable museum exhibits, and magnificent collections of books were plundered. Turned by the Nazis into a charred ruin, the Catherine Palace presented a sorry sight. Only in 16 out of the 55 elegant rooms had fragments of the interior architectural decor been preserved. Shapeless piles of stones and heaps of smoking ruins remained on the site of many pavilions. The parks suffered great damage. The Nazis destroyed more than three thousand century-old oaks, limes, aspens, and maples, and demolished bridges and dams.

Among the many units and divisions that liberated Pushkin there was the 267th independent machine-gun artillery battalion. The commander of one of the companies in this battalion, a Leningrader Nikolai Prokhorov, subsequently wrote in his memoirs: "On January 24, 1944, at 4:30 a.m. our machine-gun artillery company came out on the edge of Pushkin... The fighters from Leningrad who had often been in Pushkin could not believe their eyes. Their hearts turned cold when they saw the destruction caused by the Nazi barbarians. The houses had been turned into ruins and debris. Fires blazed all around, and tree stumps stuck out of the ground where the tops of the age-old trees of Pushkin park had once rustled. The town was dead...

Even from a distance we espied the terrible, mutilated shell of the Catherine Palace. Instead of the gilded cupola of the church all that was visible was a single wire frame on rafters. The central part of the palace had lost its roof, the windows and doors were smashed, the splendid moulded figures embellishing the façade of the building were marred... We entered the palace church through a hole in the wall. It was littered with broken motor-bikes and cannisters, and the floor was covered with fuel oil. The parquet floor of valuable woods was torn up and chopped up. The windows and frames had been shattered, and the wind blew through the church. The gilt ornamentation and sculptures had been disfigured and the iconostasis had been destroyed completely."

In the rooms of the Catherine Palace the fighters discovered mines, air bombs and shells joined together by wires. The Nazis had intended to blow up everything that had by some miracle escaped destruction. The commander of the 267th battalion mentioned this briefly in his report: "The set of explosives in the Catherine Palace was defused by the intelligence forces."

The war was still going on, but in liberated Pushkin work started on clearing the parks and ponds, and doing the first restoration work in the Catherine Palace and the pavilions. In the post-war years the Leningraders have put colossal effort into bringing the palaces and parks in Pushkin back to life. Exhibiting great concern that these extremely valuable monuments of art should be restored, the Communist Party and Soviet government allotted huge sums for the restoration work. The real scale of the restoration work can only be evaluated by those who see this magnificent palace and park ensemble today, the façades of the Catherine Palace and the park pavilions glistening with their former beauty.

The thousands of young trees planted along the avenues have now spread their branches. Rows of bushes line whimsically winding restored paths. The sculptures have been mounted on their pedestals, and the monuments to military glory have been restored.

Top specialists from the Restavrator scientific restoration association — architects and painters, sculptors and gilders, craftsmen skilled in wood and stone carving — are engaged in the restoration of the palaces and parks in Pushkin. Many hundreds of fragments of wood carving, moulding, marble, stained glass, gathered up from the territory of the parks, were used as examples in restoring the façades and interiors of the buildings. The palace's research staff made a painstaking study of the graphic and archive materials, prewar photographs and sketches with measurements. On the basis of their findings, a team of specialists headed by the architect Alexander Kedrinsky worked out a draft for the restoration of all the buildings in the ensemble, making them look just as they did when they were created. The first restored rooms of the Catherine Palace were opened to the public in 1959. Now visitors can see the Pushkin ensemble in all its glory.

The restoration of each room involved difficulties, searches and finds. For example, it seemed unthinkable to recreate the Chinese Drawing-Room, which had lost its main embellishment, its Chinese silk. However, using old photographs, the artist and restorer R. D. Slepushkina managed to paint the silk again over a period of two years. The silk, pillaged by the Nazis from the Main Drawing-Room, was reproduced at the Rosa

During the Second World War Catherine Palace was almost completely destroyed by the Nazis. View of the Main Staircase after the liberation.

Luxemburg silk factory in Moscow. In restoring the main staircase, most of the moulding had to be recreated; the parts of the marble handrail and vases that had been destroyed either had to be stuck together or carved anew; the lost paintings on the ceiling had to be replaced by similar ones. The moulded decor of the Green Dining-Room was restored and completed; the graceful china columns giving the Bed-Chamber its original look, had to be glued together; the painting on the ceiling and in the frieze of the Blue Drawing-Room had to be reproduced.

It was particularly difficult to restore the rooms created by Rastrelli, for it required masterly skill to bring to life the unrestrained fantasy of his designs. For example, it took a whole team of restorers six years to return the picture gallery to its former magnificence. Apart from the paintings, almost the whole collection of which was evacuated, everything in this room has been created anew. And now, just as formerly, you do not know what amazes you more: the colourful pattern of the parquet made from 12 types of light wood, the stoves with their hand-painted tiles, or the really fantastic composition of the gilt jambs and lintels of the doors created by the restorers from photographs. Similar complications were involved in restoring the Cavaliers' Dining-Room. The restoration of the palace is continuing.

Not only the palace and park ensembles and the wealth of objets d'art in the museum are being carefully preserved in the town of Pushkin, but also memorial buildings connected with the life and work of Nikolai Karamzin, Mikhail Lermontov, Sergei Yesenin, Alexei Tolstoy, Konstantin Fedin, Anna Akhmatova, and other outstanding figures in Russian culture.

Today, many buildings are going up in Pushkin, but the historical look of its central part is being carefully conserved. The town is continuing to develop as a town in the environs of Leningrad where the inhabitants of that city and numerous tourists can spend their leisure time.

"The average number of inhabitants is 15 thousand", a guidebook stated in 1882. Now some 90 thousand people live in Pushkin. New residential districts have been erected in the northern part of the town, where you enter it when you come from Leningrad. They form the view you get of Pushkin from a distance.

Perpetuating the best traditions of the town's formation established in the eighteenth and nineteenth centuries, Soviet architects have preserved its unique historical character with the palace and park ensemble remaining dominant in its architecture. From the railway station you can reach the palace by 371 or 382 bus. When the weather is fine, especially in autumn when Pushkin looks particularly beautiful, you can walk it, along Lenin and First of May Streets. It will take you about 30 minutes.

Places Connected with Alexander Pushkin

THE MONUMENT
TO ALEXANDER PUSHKIN

The town of Pushkin is not only famous for its remarkable palaces, gardens, and parks. Here there is much to remind you of the great Russian poet, Alexander Pushkin, the favourite and most famed poet in this country. The poet lived in Tsarskoye Selo, was fond of this cosy, little town with its splendid architectural complexes. It was here that he acquired his first friends. It was here that his gift as a poet first became evident and he started out on his career. Tsarskoye Selo and the Lyceum were recalled in his verses throughout his short lifetime.

An excursion round the places connected with the poet begins with the monument, which has become the town's symbol. The sculptor Rudolf Bach has depicted the young Pushkin, sitting on an old park bench, at a moment when he is resting or deep in thought. The young man is looking into the distance, his eyes sad and serious, his curly head resting on his hand. The statue was created in 1900 and stands in what was formerly the little garden of the Lyceum; this was part of the park fenced off so that the pupils of the Tsarskoye Selo could spend their time there in the breaks between lessons. The little garden is separated from the Lyceum building by a narrow passageway.

THE LYCEUM

The wing of the palace designed by the architect Ilya Neyelov and erected in 1789-1791, was handed over to the Lyceum in 1810 by "decree of His Imperial Majesty"; the Lyceum was a new educational establishment for a small group of extremely gifted children from the families of the gentry who "were earmarked to make an important contribution to the service of the State". It was thought that in the future they could have a hand in promoting social transformations and enlightenment in Russia and in putting progressive ideas into effect.

Statue of Alexander Pushkin near the Egyptian Gates, by Leonid Bernstam, 1912.

*Great Hall
of the Lyceum.*

The architect Vasili Stasov was commissioned to adapt the building to the needs of the future educational institution. He did not change its exterior designed by Ilya Neyelov at all, only subjecting "the building's outside to replastering".

The centre of the Lyceum's main façade is marked by a portico of four Corinthian columns. A moulded decorative frieze stretches above the windows on the second floor, and the surface of the socle's walls has been plastically worked with narrow rustication. The passageway linking the building with the Catherine Palace church has been cut by three beautifully proportioned arches.

However, during Stasov's reconstruction the interiors of the palace wing were subjected to considerable alterations. Ivan Pushchin, a friend of Push-

kin's at the Lyceum and a poet, described the Lyceum's premises in the following manner: "The lower floor housed the manager's office and the flats of the inspector, the governors, and some other officials... On the first floor there was the dining-room, the hospital and chemist's and the conference hall and chancery; the second floor, accommodated the recreation hall and the classes, the physics room, the newspape and journals room and the library in the archway linking the Lyceum with the palace by means of the choir of the palace church. And the dormitories were on the top floor."

The wing placed at the disposal of the Lyceum was supplied with furniture and other articles belonging to the Imperial Palace's Department. This is how it came to be furnished with gilt carved furniture, chairs with leather and woven seats, mirrors in gilded frames, and door curtains made from brocade taken from the walls in the palace.

By the beginning of October 1811, the Lyceum building was ready to welcome its pupils. On October 19, 1811, thirty boys aged 11 to 14 years were sitting at its desks. From that day on, October 19, the Lyceum's anniversary, became a traditional annuel fête whose spirit and bard was Pushkin. Unfortunately, the poet burned his memoirs of his Lyceum days at the end of 1825. But his unique, light and exact lines about the Lyceum have been preserved in his verses, prose and letters. The events and images of those days are also revived by numerous documents, reminiscences, and letters from the Lyceum's pupils and their mentors. The purpose of the premises, their architecture and decorative interior and furnishings and various aspects of the pupils' way of life have been retraced from scraps of information scattered about in various sources; a reliable, almost tangible, picture of life at the Lyceum has been recreated.

Today, as in the time of Pushkin, the Lyceum's entrance is in Lyceum, formerly Singers' Lane; high front steps made of wrought-iron slabs enclosed by iron railings lead up to the entrance. Double glass doors with a semi-circular upper part open into the small entrance hall. At one time, when Pushkin was a pupil here, there was a door-keeper to watch that strangers did not enter the building. Visitors would ascend the old staircase to the second floor and enter the Great Hall via the antechamber overlooking the Lyceum garden.

THE GREAT HALL

Spacious and light with its four Doric columns supporting the ceiling, its whitish-pink walls painted to look like marble, and mirrors between the windows, this hall was intended for ceremonial functions. Today, a long table covered with a red golden-fringed cloth, has been placed in the middle of the hall between the columns and rows of armchairs have been lined up. This is what it was like on that memorable day, October 19, 1811, at the solemn ceremony of the opening of the Lyceum attended by the tsar, the royal family, members of the State Council, and ministers. Ivan Pushchin wrote the following in his memoirs: "A big table covered with a red gold-fringed cloth was set up in the Lyceum hall between the columns. On that table lay the deeds of His Imperial Majesty, granted to the Lyceum. We stood to the right of the table in three rows; in front of us were the headmaster, the inspector, and the governors. To the left were the professors and the other officials of the Lyceum board. The rest of the hall was filled with rows of armchairs for the public which ended a little way away from the table."

"The granted deeds" about which Ivan Pushchin reminisces, or the Lyceum regulations, can now be seen in the exposition. They are on the table in the Great Hall, contained in a luxurious cover embroidered with gold and silk and fixed into a gilded case with the state seal.

The pupils particularly remembered the brilliant speech at the opening of the Lyceum by the future lecturer in law, Alexander Kunitsyn. In a sonorous voice, not in the least embarrassed by the tsar's presence, he spoke of the obligations of a citizen and warrior, of love for one's homeland and of one's duty to it. Kunitsyn's words about the great need to serve one's motherland became a sort of programme for providing patriotic education at the Lyceum.

The hall is especially memorable because it was precisely here that on January 8, 1815, the final examinations were held at which the fifteen-year-old Alexander Pushkin read his own verses "Reminiscenses at Tsarskoye Selo" devoted to the recent events of 1812 in the presence of the famous Russian poet Gavrila Derzhavin.

"At last they summoned me," the poet recalls. "I read my 'Reminiscences at Tsarskoye Selo', standing two paces away from Derzhavin. I haven't got the strength to describe my state of mind: when I got to the verse where I mention Derzhavin's name, my voice began to ring like an adolescent's and my heart beat with intoxicating delight... I don't remember how I finished my reading, I don't remember where I ran off to. Derzhavin was in raptures: he demanded that I be brought to him, he wanted to embrace me. They looked for me, but they didn't find me." This is how that curly, blushing teenager

passed his examination for the high title of Russian Poet with his own hymn to the victorious people in the Patriotic War of 1812.

The first graduation ceremony was held in the Great Hall on June 9, 1817. Seventeen of the school leavers opted for the civil service, and twelve chose a military career.

It should be mentioned that the Lyceum was indeed an advanced educational establishment in its time. First and foremost, the pupils here learned the art of studying on their own, of working with books, of thinking for themselves, and of interpreting history and contemporary events. Many of Pushkin's acquaintances at the Lyceum have gone down in the history of Russia: thus, Ivan Pushchin and Wilhelm Küchelbecker were active participants in the December uprising of 1825 against the tsarist autocracy and Vladimir Volkhovski, Alexander Bakunin, and Alexander Kornilov were affiliated to the Decembrists; Alexander Gorchakov became a brilliant diplomat; Fyodor Matyushkin became well known as a seafarer, Mikhail Yakovlev a composer, Anton Delvig a poet, and so forth. His contemporaries referred to the first graduates from the Lyceum as brilliant.

It is not accidental that the young poet's first recitation was devoted to the glorious feats of the Russian soldiers. The war of 1812, Napoleon's huge, almost six-hundred-thousand-strong army, which invaded Russia, the alarming news, and the military communiqués, all worried the Lyceum's pupils and greatly affected their political development. Ivan Pushchin wrote at that time, "Our Lyceum life is merging with the political age of the life of the Russian people, and the threat of 1812 is imminent."

In that disturbing year, the tremendous upsurge of patriotism seized all strata of Russian society and played an important part in the formation of the Lyceum pupils' world outlook. They were extremely upset that they could not join in the struggle to save their motherland. Pushchin recalls: "It began with us bidding all the Guards regiments farewell for they went right past the Lyceum ... Not a single tear flowed!"

Military communications, newspapers, letters from home bearing reports on military operations were usually discussed in the Newspaper Room. Its interior can be seen from the Great Hall.

THE NEWSPAPER ROOM

A round red-wood table dating from the end of the eighteenth the beginning of the nineteenth century stands in the room as well as a chess table and chairs of that time. On the tables there are reports from the scene of military operations, candlesticks, and tweezers. The oil lamps on the walls are replicas of old examples. On the maps of Europe and the hemispheres hanging on the walls the pupils traced the advance of the armies in 1812.

"The Newspaper Room was never empty," recalls Ivan Pushchin, "in the free time after or in between classes, Russian and foreign journals were read, the pupils vying with one another, the room unceasingly abuzz with talking and discussions; everything inspired a lively reaction in us: fears immediately gave way to delight as soon as there was even the slightest turn for the better. The professors came and taught us how to trace the course of operations and events, explaining things that we were not able to comprehend ourselves."

THE LYCEUM LIBRARY

A double door leads from the Great Hall into the gallery above the archway joining the Lyceum to the palace. Today the library is furnished as it was in Pushkin's time: there are card-tables of red wood, massive painted chairs with leather seats, lamps, light blue door curtains with tassels. Just as formerly the walls are painted light-blue and the ceiling is decorated with garlands.

The six book-cases contain genuine books from the Lyceum, some 700 copies of editions found here at the beginning of the 19th century. These were, as a rule, books brought by the pupils from home or books presented to the

Lyceum. There are quite a lot of books in French and German, for the Lyceum is known to have put great store by the learning of these languages as well as Latin.

From the library you can go through the Great Hall into the Intercommunicating and the Long rooms. Just as in the Newspaper room, the walls in these rooms are painted to look like green marble, and the ceilings have been white-washed. In Pushkin's time, each pupil had his own desk here for doing his homework. One of these desks stands in the Intercommunicating Room today, and on it you will see a rough copy of Pushkin's notes. On the round table in the corner to the right of the entrance lie copies of caricatures and magazines put out by the Lyceum pupils. Fencing gear of Pushkin's time is on display in the Long Room. It is noteworthy that the future poet was a first class fencer and was very fond of that graceful, lively sport.

When you leave the Long Room, you enter the classroom.

THE CLASSROOM

This is an extremely spacious, light room where all the pupils' main classes were held. Now the classroom looks just as it did originally. The walls are painted pale green, and the ceiling bears the signs of the zodiac. The blackboard stands by the wall on a tripod. The teacher's desk and platform are raised. The six school desks whose tops can be lifted are arranged in the amphitheatre of the room: three rows of two tables, each for five people. In this class the pupils had lessons given by Kunitsyn, who taught logic, psychology, morals, finance, and state laws. Clever, eloquent and well educated, he gave his lectures in a lively colourful manner, citing numerous different examples. Kunitsyn's words to the effect that when people enter society, they desire freedom and well-being, and not enslavement and poverty, that the people play a decisive part in the choice of government and the making of laws, had a tremendous influence on the formation of the pupils' moral character. It is no accident that Pushkin wrote on a copy of the book *The History of the Pugachev Mutiny* "To Alexander Petrovitch Kunitsyn from the author as a mark of profound respect and gratitude".

Pushkin's first biographer, Pavel Annenkov, wrote of the teacher of Russian literature Nikolai Koshanski, the historian Ivan Kaidanov, and the mathematician Yakov Kartsev: "It can be said without any exaggeration that all these people must be considered progressive people of the age in their field of education."

On the front desks there are summaries (copies) of the lectures taken down by Gorchakov, the pupil who made the best progress in his studies at the Lyceum. On the wall pier between the

*Monument to Alexander Pushkin in the Lyceum
Garden, by Rudolph Bach, 1900.*

Lyceum, a view from the back.

Classroom.

Singing classroom.

Lyceum Library.

Alexander Pushkin's dormitory.

Lyceum Great Hall.

*Kitayeva's Summer Cottage:
drawing-room (top),
Alexander Pushkin's study.*

Autumn in Pushkin.

windows which look out over the Lyceum garden, hangs the pupils' timetable for the day. Bell rings to get up at 6 a.m., from 7 a.m. till 9 a.m.—classes, at 9 a.m.—tea and a bun and first walk until 10 a.m.; from 10 a.m. till 12 a.m.—classes, and from mid-day till 1 p.m.—the second walk. At one o'clock the pupils had lunch, from 2 p.m. till 3 p.m.—calligraphy, from 3 p.m. till 5 p.m.—classes continued; at 5 p.m. tea was served and then they took a walk till 6 p.m. Supper was served at 9 o'clock in the evening and lights went out at 10 p.m.

THE PHYSICS ROOM

The pupils had lessons in the Physics Room, the Drawing and Singing Rooms, which come one after the other on your excursion. For those times, the physics room had excellent equipment kept in cupboards along the walls adjacent to the classroom. On the table in the middle of the room there is a class register from which you will see that Alexander Pushkin was not distinguished for his exceptional zeal in the sciences, especially in the exact ones but invariably got good marks in Russian literature. At that time, incidentally, the top mark was "one" and not "five" as it is now in the Soviet Union.

THE DRAWING
AND SINGING CLASSROOMS

Every day three or four pupils did some drawing and moulding. Some of their works are on display in the room, two of them "A Dog with a Bird in Its Teeth" and "A Kvass* Seller" by Alexander Pushkin. It is thought that Pushkin copied the head of the seller from his fellow-pupil Pavel Yudin.

* A Russian fermented drink made from rye bread.—*Tr.*

In the Singing Room, a small light room with two windows, the pupils gathered round the clavichords, which still stand in the room. On the top of the clavichords you will see the music to the Lyceum's farewell song "Six Years" with words by Pushkin's close friend Anton Delvig, who was distinguished for his unusual gift for poetry.

33

THE DORMITORIES

From the Singing Room a door leads on to a staircase going up to the third floor where visitors find themselves in a long vaulted corridor ending with a glazed door on both sides. The dormitories are situated along each side of the corridor. They are separated from one another and also from the corridor by partitions, which fall short of the ceiling and divide each window in half so that each bedroom has half a window. The room's simple furnishings consist of an iron bedstead covered with a blanket, a chest of drawers, a desk, a chair, a small washstand of imitation red-wood with a mirror. On the desk there is an ink-pot, a candlestick, and tweezers. At one end of the corridor there is a room for the governor on duty in which articles from the end of the eighteenth and the beginning of the nineteenth centuries are arranged. "At nights night-lights were placed in all the archways in the corridor. The fellow on duty would pace the corridor with measured stride," wrote Ivan Pushchin.

The semi-darkness of the corridor with the high arches of its vaults, the small windows of the pupils' rooms, the strict order of the day, life confined within the walls of the Lyceum, for the pupils were not allowed to leave it even during the holidays, made school life reminiscent of a monastic routine. It is not accidental that the pupils called their bedrooms "cells". Later on, in his novel in verse, *Eugene Onegin*, Pushkin recalls:

My student cell was filled with light:
The Muse opened a banquet there
Of all the schemes that boys hold dear
Extolling what gives them delight,
And our home country's glorious past,
And dreams that make the heart beat fast.

Room 14. On a black plaque above the door next to the number there is an inscription "Alexander Pushkin". On the board of the room next to it, No. 13, there is the name of Pushkin's friend, Ivan Pushchin. The muffled whispering of the friends could be heard far into the night. This is how Pushchin recalls those nights: "As his neighbour (on the other side of him there was a blank wall) often, when practically everyone had fallen asleep, I would chat to him under my breath through the partition about some foolish happening of that day; here I could see quite clearly that, owing to a sense of delicacy, he attributed some kind of importance to any silly thing that happened, and it worried him. Together, we smoothed out some of the ups and downs as well as we could, although we didn't always manage it." That friendship forged at the Lyceum continued throughout their lives. The poet described Pushchin as "My first friend, my invaluable friend".

Kitayeva's Summer Cottage.

Pushkin was fond of the Lyceum, he loved his friends, and he dedicated to it one of his splendid poems "October 19th" (1825):

My friends, this our alliance is most fair!
Eternal, indivisible as the soul—
Unshakeable, free, with no cares at all,
It grew up in the friendly Muses' care.
Wherever we are led by life and fortune,
Wherever fate decrees that we must go,
We'll be the same: to us, the whole world's foreign,
Our proper home is Tsarskoye Selo.

KITAYEVA'S SUMMER COTTAGE

Ten to fifteen minutes walk from the Lyceum, on the corner of Pushkinskaya (formerly Kolpinskaya) and Vasenko (formerly the Kusmin Road) Streets stands a small single-storey house with a semi-circular glazed veranda and also a semi-circular glazed mezzanine floor. The memorial plaque on the façade reads "Alexander Pushkin lived here in 1831". Today the cottage houses the Pushkin Museum.

The cottage, which belonged to Anna Kitayeva, the widow of a court valet, in 1831, was built in 1828. At that time, the whole of the corner part was taken up by a spacious open veranda with columns, and above it, on the mezzanine floor, there was an open balcony. Nestling amidst the luxuriant greenery of trees and bushes, this cottage was typical of those in Tsarskoye Selo in the first half of the 19th century. In spite of

*Portrait of Alexander
Pushkin, engraving by Nikolai
Utkin from the oil painting by
Orest Kiprensky, 1827.*

*Portrait of Natalia Pushkin,
oil painting by Alexander
Bryullov, 1831.*

its closeness to the capital, Tsarskoye Selo breathed the cosiness and tranquility of the countryside. Pushkin asked his friend, Pyotr Pletnev, to rent a cottage just like this one for him where he could enjoy "inspiring seclusion". The poet was very pleased with the cottage. When he had settled down in Kitayeva's cottage, he wrote in one of his letters: "We live quietly and cheerfully here as if we are in the depths of the countryside."

The summer of 1831 was a happy one for Pushkin. On February 18, 1831, he married Natalya Goncharova, the belle of Moscow society, with whom he was passionately in love ("I am married and happy," he wrote to Pyotr Pletnev a week later). On May 25th, the young couple moved to the cottage at Tsarskoye Selo. It was not accidental that Pushkin chose this place to start a new life, for he wanted to experience this welcome change in his life "amidst pleasant memories" of the Lyceum and his friends there.

Pushkin rented a suite of seven small rooms from Kitayeva and a room on the mezzanine floor which he made his study. The walls of the rooms were painted green, dark and light blue, grey and pale yellow, thus adding them space and light; the furniture was arranged freely, and the cottage was cosy and quiet.

Today six of the rooms have been made to look just as they did then, including the study. Your tour of the poet's house begins in the entrance hall where there is a small exposition telling you something about the memorial part of the house beforehand.

The next room is the Pantry, which has red-wood furniture. On the little table in the corner stands a copper-plated nickel samovar, and the sideboard holds chinaware of the end of the 18th century. On the table by the door you will see a book containing hand-written recipes of the beginning of the nineteenth century.

The door from the pantry will take you into the Dining-Room, a small room with two windows looking onto the street. There is a mirror in the pier, and on the wall to the left of the door hang portraits of Pushkin's parents and his sister Olga. On the needlework table in the far corner from the door stands a china vase dating from the end of the 18th century. There is a white tablecloth on the dinner table, and the armchairs and chairs are upholstered with dark-red brocade.

The most spacious room in the cottage is the parlour. Oval-shaped, its four windows now look out onto the glazed veranda. In Pushkin's time, the veranda was an open one, and people would enter the cottage and the parlour across the veranda. The small amount of furniture in the room consisting of an oval table with four chairs round it and a couch by the fireplace, is made of Karelian birchwood. On the table you can see women's fashions in the year

*"Alexander Pushkin",
watercolour by an unknown
artist, first third of 19th
century.*

1832 and pages from an album of embroidery patterns. Pushkin's friends often got together in this room; the poet Vasili Zhukovsky, who was well known in Russia, the very young Nikolai Gogol, in whom Pushkin already spotted a great writer when he read *Evenings on a Farm Near Dikanka* for the first time, Alexandra Rosset-Smirnova, a maid of honour at the royal court, who was distinguished for her beauty and wit. Here his friends celebrated Natalya Pushkin's nineteenth birthday. She was 13 years younger than her husband and was one of the most beautiful women of her day. Pushkin called her his Madonna, and in Tsarskoye Selo she was often referred to as Psyche. She strove to be a good housewife and assistant to her husband. It was precisely in the summer of that year that Pushkin's wife "was noticed" at court and she was offered the position of maid of honour to the empress.

The next room, which has one window, was Natalya Pushkin's **Boudoir**. The furnishings consist of a dressing table, a little chest of drawers, and two chairs. To the left of the door hangs a portrait of the young housewife by Alexander Bryullov.

Of interest in the room, which serves as a **Bedroom** where an interior typical of those of the first half of the nineteenth century has been recreated, are the extracts copied by Natalya Pushkin from the works by the French historians Guizot and Menier which were banned in Pushkin's time.

The poet's **Study** on the mezzanine floor is, like the parlour, oval-shaped.

Its simple furnishings consist of a large round table in front of the couch on which manuscripts, paper, exercise books, a simple ink-pot and quill pens lie. Next to it on a small table there is a decanter with water, a jar of the poet's favourite gooseberry jam. Books are scattered about everywhere, on the table, the shelves and the floor. There are no curtains at the window. According to the reminiscences of Pushkin's friends, he was not troubled by the heat. As a rule, he worked in the morning after he had had tea. At Kitayeva's cottage, he wrote the fairy-tales "About the Tsar Saltan", "About the Priest and his Man-Servant Balda", the tale "Roslavlev", and numerous verse such as "What They Celebrate Most at the Lyceum", "Echo", "To the Slanderers of Russia", "The Anniversary of Borodino", and others. Here he wrote Onegin's letter to Tatiana which he later inserted in the eighth chapter of the famous novel in verse *Eugene Onegin*.

Portraits of Zhukovsky and Rosset-Smirnova in water-colours and an engraving of Gogol hang on the wall above the couch.

Pushkin's quiet, measured life in Tsarskoye Selo did not last for long. A cholera epidemic flared up in St. Petersburg in June, and in mid-July the court moved to Tsarskoye Selo to avoid infection. In Pushkin's own words, everything there immediately began "to seethe", and Tsarskoye Selo "was turned into the capital". With the arrival of the courtiers, the poet was no longer able to enjoy those wonderful secluded walks in the Catherine Park.

"Poet Vasili Zhukovsky",
water-colour by Pyotr Sokolov.

"Tsarskoye Selo can drive you mad; it's much easier to find seclusion in St. Petersburg," Pushkin now wrote in one of his letters. Life at court was beyond the poet's means, distracted him from his work, and at the end of October the Pushkins left Tsarskoye Selo.

Besides the Pushkin exposition in the two rooms on the ground floor in Kitayeva's cottage, there are also exhibitions devoted to the historian and writer Nikolai Karamzin and the poet Vasili Zhukovsky, who were of no small importance in the life of Alexander Pushkin.

* * *

In the north wing (also called the Church wing) of the Catherine Palace there is the Literature and Monograph exposition of the All-Union Pushkin Museum, whose 27 rooms contain more than 1,500 exhibits. Here you can see depictions of Pushkin made during his lifetime, of his relatives and friends, and genuine objects d'art dating from the beginning of the 19th century, and the poet's personal belongings and books. Your attention is sure to be commanded by the copies of Pushkin's manuscripts made on old paper.

The Catherine
Palace
The Parks

THE CATHERINE PALACE

During this excursion, which lasts approximately one hour, you will see restored interiors by Rastrelli, Cameron, Stasov, and Monighetti in twenty-two rooms, and also expositions of materials on the history and restoration of the palace. All the rooms are on the first floor and the service premises of the palace are on the ground floor, including the cloakroom. You enter the museum by the main entrance from the French garden.

THE MAIN STAIRCASE

Your tour of the palace begins with the main staircase situated in the very centre of the building. This staircase was created in 1861 by the architect Ippolito Monighetti, who strove to make it blend stylistically with the existing Rastrelli interiors.

The carved hand rail framing the white marble steps, the stucco decorations in the form of volutes, scrolls and garlands on the walls, the decorative sculptures are reminiscent of drawings of the luxurious ornamentation in rooms of the mid-18th century. The special glow and colourfulness of the interior is imparted by the brightly coloured decorative dishes and vases of ancient Chinese and Japanese china dotted along the walls. They contrast with the whiteness of the walls, the marble of the steps, and the railing of the staircase, beautifully enhancing the palette of colour of the paintings on the ceiling.

During the Second World War and the Nazi occupation the decorations on the main staircase were destroyed by fire. The paintings by Italian artists of the 18th century were replaced by stylistically analogous ones of similar size by masters of the 18th-century Italian school: "The Judgement of Paris" and "Jupiter and Calisto", which came from the Hermitage, the USSR's biggest art museum, and by the work of an unknown Italian artist "Aeneas and Venus" presented as a gift to the Catherine Palace by A. P. Tikhomirov, an engineer from Leningrad.

From the landings of the main staircase you get a splendid view of the Catherine and Alexander parks.

*Central gate of the main
courtyard.*

THE EXHIBITION HALLS

From the main staircase you will go to the exhibition halls. At one time, these rooms formed part of the so-called Small Suite, which was located parallel to the main suite and consisted of the apartment of the tsar's family. These apartments were decorated in a rather more modest manner than the reception rooms. Now the Small Suite is being restored to house various exhibitions. At the first exposition you can see materials telling you about the main periods in the creation of the palace. Portraits of the architects Rastrelli, Cameron, and Stasov, hang on the walls. Your attention is bound to be attracted by the model of the Great Palace made by the architect Alexei Kvasov in 1740, the picture "A View of the Great Palace" (1760-1761) by the artist Friedrich Hartman Barisien and an engraving of the drawing by Mikhail Makhaev "Panorama of the Great Palace".

A special section shows you how the Catherine Palace was transformed into a history and art museum in the early post-war years. In the exposition you can see the decree of the Soviet of People's Commissars on the nationalisation of the property of the Romanovs, the first ticket into the museum on June 9, 1918, the visitor's book and photographs of the first visitors to the museum.

The exposition, in the second hall is devoted to the events of the Second World War and the restoration of the palace and park ensemble in Pushkin in the post-war years. Documentary photographs describe the organized evacuation, by decision of the Soviet government, to the eastern regions—to Siberia and the Urals, of twenty thousand exhibits, and the tremendous destruction wrought by the Nazis to these world famous monuments of Russian culture. Lithographs by the artist V. Vasilyev depict the town of Pushkin in ruins, after it was liberated from Nazi occupation in January 1944.

A considerable section of the exposition contains materials on the tremendous restoration work, frequently unique, carried out in the post-war years, as a result of which the palaces and parks of Pushkin have been returned to their former state. Fragments of the plans to restore the Catherine Palace are presented, as well as sketches for the recreation of the painted ceiling of the Great Hall, the surviving store tiles and those recreated by the restorers, and the instruments of the carvers and gilders.

Photographs have captured the complicated work of the modern carvers who had to master 18th-century carving techniques and work out methods of replacing the missing fragments.

The exposition gives an idea of the high professional standard of the painters, gilders, moulders, and parquet layers whose labour and talent have revived the magnificence of the Great Hall.

THE GREAT HALL

The Great Hall or the Light Gallery is the most spacious premises in the palace, its main hall. The architect Bartholomeo Rastrelli accentuated this not only with the splendour of the decor but also with its magnificent dimensions, for the hall is 860 sq.m. in area. Official receptions and balls were usually held here during which 696 candles were burned in the carved sconces in front of the mirrors. Rastrelli's design for the interior is an extremely simple one: the hall is rectangular in plan, 47 metres long, and includes a suite of elegant rooms situated along the length of it. This design for the interior is characteristic of this architect's work. However, in the decor of the hall Rastrelli used a wide variety of artistic methods: golden lace of carved decoration, around the huge glazed doors and mirrors creating the illusion of more space, the richly decorated plafond taking your glance upwards to the boundless expanses of the sky, the complicated dynamic design of the gilded wall carving. The unique beauty of this magical decoration, bathed by rays of light from the doors and windows, creates a sensation of festiveness.

The main ornamentation on the walls of the Great Hall is woodcarving. One hundred and thirty Russian craftsmen, using Rastrelli's sketches and patterns by Dunker worked the wooden decoration of the Great Hall in such a way that every detail of the ornamentation was a work of art. In the hands of such masters as Pyotr Valyukhin, Dmitry Sakulisnoy, Ivan Sukhoy, and others the lime-tree wood did as it were come to life, being transformed into fiery cupids with palettes and lyre in the upper tiers of the windows, then graceful gilded female figures, Caryatids mounted in the door frames. The fanciful carved ornament characteristic of baroque style splays out around the windows and mirrors like golden streams.

The numerous mirrors reflected and reiterated the complicated rhythm and the dynamic nature of the gilded carving, and the frieze on the gigantic ceiling painted by the well-known Italian master of decorative art Giuseppe Valeriani with the help of Antonio Peresinotti and the Russian artists Alexei and Yefim Belsky, Ivan and Pyotr Firsov, and others.

The ceiling "The Triumph of Russia" glorified in allegorical form Russia's successes on the battlefield and the flourishing of its science and art. The centre of the composition consisting of three parts is a female figure, the personification of Russia. She is depicted very dynamically, against the background of a boundless sky and fluffy clouds, which creates the illusion that the hall is of unusual height. The sensation that the interior of the hall is boundless is intensified by its design which does as it were frame the frieze. The colonnade towering upwards, the niches, the vases, the garlands of flowers, and the painted balconies have

Great Hall: carved decoration around the doors.

been worked in conformity with all the laws of perspective.

The Great Hall suffered tremendous damage during the war. Large shells destroyed the roof, the ceiling and part of the walls facing onto the park. A considerable section of the ceiling and the carved wall decorations were totally destroyed together with all the mirrors, and the decorative parquet designed by Rastrelli. What remained of the decor required serious restoration.

Using the surviving carving as a model for creating the main compositions and also photographs and drawings, the sculptor Lilya Shvedskaya, the stucco moulder Vera Zaitseva, the woodcarvers Victor Bogdanov, Anatoli Vinogradov, Yury Kozlov, Alexei Kochuyev, and others were able to restore the fanciful carved ornamentation in all its complicated detail as accurately as possible. The thin gilt frond again wound its way along the walls.

When recreating the central part of the ceiling of the Great Hall the artists and restorers made use of the description of its first author Giuseppe Valeriani and also of a number of documentary materials. As luck would have it, the sides of the ceiling were discovered on the ceiling of the Throne Hall of the Engineers' Castle in Leningrad during restoration in 1954.

The decorative parquet was restored from Rastrelli's own design, the only fragment of it being found in a German dug-out. Its geometrical design, consisting of large pointed figures, was built up on the contrast of dark and light oak.

Now the Great Hall, in which the huge expanses and the effect of perspective, the magical play of reflections, the gilt carving and paintings combine, again looks like something out of a fairy-tale. The revived works of art of the 18th century are a real feat on the part of Soviet restorers, the result of their 20-year-long efforts.

THE MAIN SUITE

Adjacent to the Great Hall are the rooms of Rastrelli's Main Suite. In the mid-17th century these rooms were mainly intended for official receptions. The festivities and solemn ceremonies attended by many people were held in the Great Hall and its antechambers in which, as mentioned previously, the courtiers awaited the entrance of the empress. A small circle of selected guests were received in the Amber Room and the Portrait Gallery and also in the "Column" Rooms (see further on).

The rooms of the suite were decorated in true baroque style with lace-like ornamentation on the walls covered with white brocade, luxurious gilt frames, high tiled stoves with cobalt drawings, an abundance of mirrors in gilt carved frames.

During the Second World War these rooms were completely destroyed.

The research staff of the Catherine Palace had to do some hard research work to determine what the interior decor of the main suite was like in the mid-18th century, to select the corresponding furniture, paintings, light fittings, and other objects of applied art since inventories of the furnishings of other palaces of that time had not been preserved and no one had an accurate idea what the initial interior was like.

The restoration of the carved ornamentation in the suite was particularly difficult since not even a fragment of the original carving had survived. However, the skilful carvers of the Leningrad Restavrator association attained extraordinary results, using graphic materials, prewar photographs and other archive sources, and having mastered the methods of wood-carving for which the decorative carvers of the 18th century were famous. Now even specialists cannot distinguish the renewed carving from the original. Just as in the ornamentation of the 18th century, today the whimsical lines, the stylized leaves and flowers interwoven into amazing decorative patterns, so typical of the epoch of Rastrelli baroque and at the same time realistically done tubby little boys, "putti", are nowhere repeated in the patterns. The individuality of each carver is evident in his awareness of form, material and volume. The enevitable deviations from the model do not in any way ruin the harmony of the ornamentation in the suite.

In recreating the interiors of the palace, the restorers and artists had to ensure the stylistic unity of the architectural and decorative ornamentation of the objects in its interior decor, and make them true monuments of art of a certain historical epoch. Thus, today the halls of Rastrelli's suite are furnished in baroque style with plasticity of forms, gentle wavy contours and an abundance of gilded carved details. The light gilded chairs are upholstered with expensive fabrics of refined colour and design and have typical curving intricate oval backs. The chests of drawers, writing desks and bureaus with numerous secret compartments are decorated with ornamentation in gilded bronze, brass, and mosaics.

The consoles covered with rich carving and the big full-length mirrors in luxurious carved frames are not only decorative but produce an optical effect, making the premises look larger and more complicated in outlay.

The gracefully shaped vases and chalices with the fine intricate ornamentation, and objets d'art by Chinese craftsmen, harmonize well with the baroque interior. The collecting of Chinese porcelain, laquered objects and various decorative articles was a common practice in Russia in the 18th century.

During the conflagration in the palace the brocade wall-papers in the suite were completely destroyed. Yet again the Palace's scientific staff plunged into a scientific quest, studying the works of the West European silk fabric art of the 17th and 18th centuries, the fabrics produced by the Yusupov factory specially for the palaces of Russian grandees and also the remains of the upholstery which had survived. Their search was crowned with success, for the design of the old white patterned brocade was restored.

Then more than one and a half thousand square metres of this decorative fabric were manufactured at the Scientific Restoration workshops in Moscow on handlooms.

The picturesque ceilings of the suite have been restored from pre-war photographs, similar ceilings and archive sources; in their time these ceilings were created by the 17th- and 18th-century Italian and Russian schools, taking subjects from ancient mythology. A complex selection of parquets of different coloured woods was also recreated from old drawings.

In 1969, the restoration of the Cavaliers' Dining-Room was completed, and this is where you enter the main suite.

THE CAVALIERS' DINING-ROOM

The windows of the Cavaliers Dining-Room, which is situated between the main staircase and the Great Hall, faced onto the courtyard. The room is decorated with the golden lace of ornamental carving on the walls, carved gilded candelabra and a whimsical carved composition with fantastic trees and hunting equipment above the door.

The multi-tier tiled stove with its cobalt drawings, miniature columns, niches and open-work cornice is of special interest.

The subject of the ceiling painted by an unknown artist of the Russian school of the mid-18th century is borrowed from Greek mythology. The picture allegorically depicts the rising of the sun, the god of the sun Helios, the goddess of dawn Eos and figures personifying the seasons of the year. The painting is framed by moulded medallions and painted insets.

The baroque style chairs made according to old examples of baroque are a perfect match for the carved ornamentation on the walls. The palace furniture of the mid-18th century is known to have been manufactured from models by Johann Dunker, who usually used Rastrelli's sketches.

Today, copying the fashion of the 18th century the gilded chairs and carved console tables under the mirrors are placed along the walls and the gilt console table in the centre of the hall has a marble top.

On the other side of the main staircase there is the Main Dining-Room symmetrical to the Cavaliers Dining-Room.

THE STATE DINING-ROOM

Official receptions were held in this room. The table in the form of the monogram of the Empress Elizabeth I, a unique, so-called hunters' china dinner service made in the 1760s at the imperial china factory in St. Petersburg, and the gilded carved console tables and chairs speak of the especially luxurious banquets.

The paintings on the walls of the State Dining-Room are part of the collection of the artist Johannes Groot, whose main subject was hunting. The painted ceiling "The Triumph of Apollo", a copy made in the 19th century from the well-known 18th-century artist Guido Reni, is of interest.

Just as in the other rooms of the suite in one corner of the main dining-room there is a large tiled stove with cobalt drawing on the figured tiles.

THE CRIMSON AND GREEN "COLUMN" ROOMS

The architect Rastrelli, when rebuilding the palace, strove to introduce variety into the architectural and decorative ornamentation of its interiors. This is how the two "column" rooms came into being, the walls of which were divided up by pilasters (or "columns") of transparent glass inlaid with crimson and green.

In the Crimson Column Room your attention will be attracted by the restored painting on the tiled stove depicting people of different strata in the 18th century. Noteworthy here too is the ceiling with a painting by an unknown Italian artist of the end of the 17th century depicting Alexander the Great and the family of the Persian king Darius III.

In the Green Column Room a modern artist Valeri Lednev recreated the painted ceiling, a picture by the 18th century Italian artist Stefano Torelli "The Military Leader at Rest Hears the Call of the Muses".

At the end of the 18th century high society lovers of card games used to gather in the Crimson Column Room with a pentagonal gaming-table in its centre.

Among the furnishings of the Column Rooms there are unique works of applied art of the mid-18th century: a bureau, intricately inlaid with various types of wood, the work of the well-known German craftsman from the town Neiwied, Abraham Roentgen, a writing-desk with a depiction of the Moscow Kremlin on the front of it made by the serf craftsman Nikifor Vasilyev, a chest of drawers of selected wood, English work of the 18th century, and a French clock of gilt bronze.

THE PORTRAIT GALLERY

This hall which is the next in the suite after the Green Column Room acquired its name because of the portraits of the two empresses who owned the palace, Catherine I, and Elizabeth, whose portraits hang there.

During the war the furnishing of the Portrait Gallery which had been preserved for two centuries disappeared. However, the two sofas with carved, fancifully patterned backs, the gilded baroque chairs, which had once stood there, made from sketches by Rastrelli, were restored by Soviet restorers from drawings. The portraits of Catherine I and Elizabeth painted by the artists Ivan Adolsky and Heinrich Bucholtz which had been preserved in evacuation were returned to their age-old places. The carvers and restorers even recreated the frames of the portraits with their intricate gilded carvings.

The plafond of the Portrait Gallery is a multi-figure composition, inserted into an oval, allegorically depicting parts of the world, the gods of Olympus and nymphs reclining in the fluffy clouds. The overall gamma of colour of the work is built up on the contrasts of rich reds, greens and yellows, soft silvers and blues. The big spaces between the individual groups of figures against the luminous background give you the impression of boundless space. The dynamics of the composition, the free moulding of the shape, the complex spatial structure, and the uniqueness of the foreshortening make it possible to suppose that the painter of the "Olympus" ceiling was the outstanding Venetian artist and decorator of the 18th century Giovanni Tiepolo.

From the Portrait Gallery visitors enter the world-famous Amber Room.

THE AMBER ROOM

In 1701, Friedrich IV, the King of Denmark, recommended the Prussian king Friedrich I that his court carver and amber polisher Gottfried Wolfram should make an amber room. It is known that from 1707 to 1712 the architect Andreas Schlüter, and the Danzig amber craftsmen Ernst Schacht and Gottfried Tussaud worked on amber panels. The twenty-two amber panels made by them were set up in one of the rooms of the Berlin Palace Mon Bijou where they attracted the attention of Peter the Great. In 1716, when the treaty of alliance with Russia was signed, the king Friedrich Wilhelm I presented the amber room to Peter the Great as a diplomatic gift. The amber panels were initially mounted in Peter the Great's Summer Palace where some rooms had elegant decor. Then they were set up in a study in the Winter Palace. From 1755 onwards the panels of "sunny stone" adorned one of the rooms in the main suite of the Catherine Palace for almost two hundred years.

The amber panels, varying in size and shape and covering an area of more than 25 square metres consist of polished amber of different hues, ranging from light blazing topaz to light lemon-coloured amber. Obviously, each piece of amber was polished individually. When inserted in the panels they did not correspond in height giving a picturesque play of sparkling light, of glittering radiance.

The noble yellowish brown gamma of amber mosaics with its warm transparent and golden hues is enhanced by the skilfully added amber frames, garlands, the heads of ancient gods, coats of arms, crowns, monograms, and whole scenes from the Bible, also carved in amber.

Rastrelli particularly displayed his skill as a decorator in the decor of the Amber Room. The hall in the Catherine Palace where the panels were mounted was considerably higher than the one in the Berlin Palace, so there was not enough amber. Therefore, striving to preserve the colour gamma of the hall, the architect ordered that a piece of canvas should be stretched across the remaining wall, painted to look like amber and decorated with luxurious gilded carving. Rastrelli was able to make the fantastic amber composition blend splendidly into the baroque interior of the hall of the main suite with its mirror-like pilasters, extremely fine carved gilt ornamentation on the walls and its mosaic pictures of agate and jasper. These attributes of baroque in the decor of the Amber Room not only forged a link between it and the other main rooms in the palace but also formed a background for the beauty, richness of colour and jewellery-like precision of the unique amber composition. Numerous descriptions of the Amber Room in memoirs and historical literature refer to it as "a fairy-tale work", "the eighth wonder of the world", "the amber poem", and "the marvel of the reign of Elizabeth". Rastrelli himself pronounced "this work of art of sunny stone to be an example of the inventiveness and creative festiveness".

When the Nazis occupied Pushkin during the war they removed the contents of the Amber Room to the former capital of East Prussia, Königsberg, where it was registered under No. 200 of 5 December, 1941, in the "list of gifts to the Prussian Museum". The amber panels were occasionally shown to a small circle of people. But, in 1944, when the victorious advance of the Soviet troops to the West began the Nazis dismantled the contents of the room and packed them into crates. No one knows what happened to this remarkable monument, and the search for it continues to this day.

At the moment restoration work is still going on in the Amber Room. Just as in the 18th century there is the frieze painted to look like amber, the restored gilded carved ornamentation on the walls and the newly-laid patterned parquet of valuable woods. The artists Yacob Kazakov and Boris Lebedev have recreated the painted plafond "The Wedding of Chronos" from a sketch by an unknown artist of the 18th-century Italian school which is preserved in the Hermitage.

In July 1979, the Council of Ministers of the RSFSR adopted a decision to revive this unique monument. Masters of the Restavrator association were commissioned to do this. The amber of which more than six tonnes is needed was delivered to Pushkin from the Yantarny (Amber) quarry in the Kaliningrad region. The amber craftsmen are creating the corresponding amber colour gamut, seeking methods of mounting the amber on wooden panels and ways of working the sunny stone.

Thus, the Amber Room is being reborn.

At the present time, you can see a model of the amber panels in the museum's exhibition which is one fifth of its actual size. On display here there are also amber mosaic caskets, carved snuff-boxes, chessmen, and goblets received as gifts from German kings and electors in the 18th century.

The door of the Amber Room leads into the Picture Gallery.

THE PICTURE GALLERY

This hall, 180 square metres in size, is one of the most considerable and elegant interiors in the palace in the richness of its architecture and artistic decor. In the 18th century it was used for official receptions, banquets and concerts more than any of the other halls. The sessions of "the Conference of the Courtiers of Most Exalted Rank" were held here during the Seven-Year War, and in the summer of 1757 there was an official reception here to mark the delivery to Tsarskoye Selo of the banners and keys of the defeated Prussian towns.

Designed by Rastrelli the interior of the hall is fantastically magnificent. The colourful paintings on the walls and plafond creating a sonorous, noble note, the glistening gilding of the luxurious carved portals, the cobalt decorations on the tiles of the tall stoves and the coloured wood of the figured parquet, are combined harmoniously.

The valuable collection of works by outstanding masters of European painting of the 17th and early 18th centuries play an important part in the decor.

The collection in the Picture Gallery has been built up on the basis of the Prague collection of paintings acquired on the orders of the empress for the palace's Picture Gallery in 1745 by the artist Georg Christoph Grooth. On the evidence of the artist himself, he acquired 112 "rare paintings by the best masters" in Prague.

After Rastrelli had created the special picture gallery, works were added to the collection which had formerly hung in the different premises of the Tsarskoye Selo palace, and also in Peterhof. The selection of the pictures and their arrangement into the symmetrical hanging pattern common at that time was done by the painter and restorer Lucas Pfanzelt.

A considerable part of the collection (114 out of 130 paintings) has survived to our day since the most valuable works were evacuated right at the beginning of the Nazi invasion. Nevertheless, in restoring the decor of the Picture Gallery in the post-war years the palace's scientific staff had to do a great deal of work to retain the integrity of the interior decor when replacing the sixteen lost works. Pictures similar in their subject, style and tone from the stocks of the Hermitage and other Leningrad museums were used to recreate the original hanging pattern. The 18th-century plafond, a copy of the ceiling by Gasparo Diziani on the main staircase in the Winter Palace in Leningrad harmonizes with the general colour scheme of the walls.

Particularly valuable among the paintings are those by well-known Dutch and Flemish masters. Your attention will be attracted by the landscapes of Jan Both in golden colours, the architectural compositions of Emanuel de Witte which are distinguished for their colour contrast, the realistic genre scenes of Adriaen van Ostade and David Teniers the younger, the still lifes by Jan David de Hem and Jan Feit. There are also extremely dynamic and highly impressive pictures by Flemish masters such as "The Allegory" by Theodor van Thulden "Storm of the Town" by Palamedes, and the 18th-century copy of the work by Rubens "Rape of the Sabine Women".

The paintings by the Italian artists Luca Giordano and Antonio Balestra are distinguished for their bright decoration.

Among the French masters the pictures by the 18th-century artist Jacques Blanchard who was called the French Tiziano for his unusually rich palette

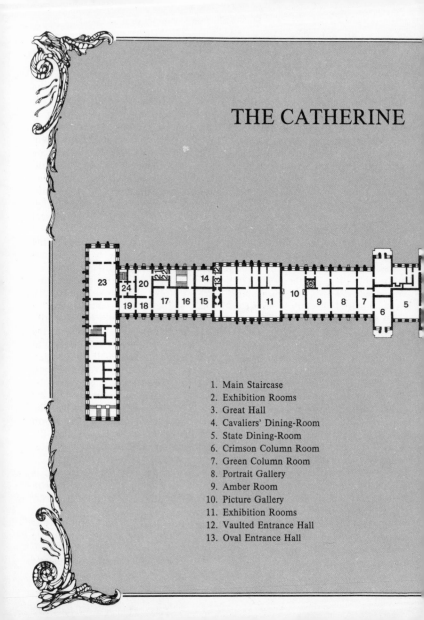

THE CATHERINE

1. Main Staircase
2. Exhibition Rooms
3. Great Hall
4. Cavaliers' Dining-Room
5. State Dining-Room
6. Crimson Column Room
7. Green Column Room
8. Portrait Gallery
9. Amber Room
10. Picture Gallery
11. Exhibition Rooms
12. Vaulted Entrance Hall
13. Oval Entrance Hall

PALACE

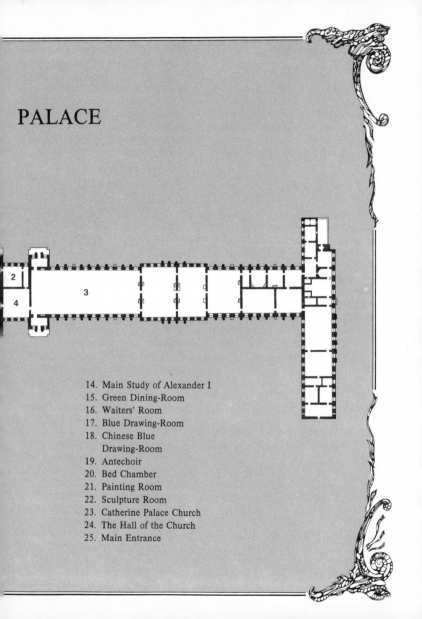

stands out among the French masters.

The collection in the Picture Gallery also includes two paintings by the French artist Pierre-Denis Martin, "The Battlefield of Poltava" and "The Battle at Lesnaya" painted specially for Peter the Great.

The collection of paintings in the Catherine Palace not only demonstrates the variety of genres and the characteristic features of the schools of painting in Western Europe in the 17th and early 18th centuries but also testifies to the development in the Russian culture of the mid-18th century of secular art and reveals Russia's cultural ties with other countries.

THE EXHIBITION ROOMS

Adjacent to the Picture Gallery are several rooms of the small suite which now serve as exhibition rooms housing expositions devoted to the construction of the Catherine Palace by the outstanding masters of classicism of the end of the 18th and early 19th centuries, Charles Cameron and Vasili Stasov. The exhibitions give a general description of the interiors in classical style, revealing its artistic ideals in architecture and decorative applied art.

The first exhibition room contains works of applied art and furnishings from the Cameron rooms which had not survived in the southern part of the palace. The objects from the interiors were evacuated right at the beginning of the war.

The water-colours exhibited allow you to see what the Cameron rooms looked like, distinguished as they were by strict symmetry, harmonious proportions, clarity and congruousness of architectural forms. In the hangings along the walls, the picturesque insets in the ceilings and in the friezes, the silk upholstery and the bronze decoration of the armchairs and the large mirrors ornamented with bronze you can see all the components of classical style depicted in the water-colours.

Copying antique examples and simultaneously using various decorative methods and materials such as stained glass, porcelain, bronze, various types of coloured stone, Cameron attains exceptional grace and refinement in the architecture of these rooms. These features are also characteristic of the furnishings and decorative applied art in the room. Thus, the influence of antiquity makes itself felt in the shape and decoration on the two torchiers shaped like stained glass columns with Doric capitals made at the St. Petersburg state glass factory in the second half of the 18th century.

The unique suite of gilt furniture from the workshop of the famous French cabinet-maker Georges Jacob is characteristic of classicism. This furniture which is distinguished for the strictness of its proportions and the preciseness of its forms was popular for a long time in Europe, right up to the 1830s. The Cameron rooms in the southern part of the palace also included in their decor paintings by the artist Hubert Robert "Ruins" and a decorative painted panel with a view of Rome exhibited here.

During the excursion you can see the restored interiors created by Cameron in the northern part of the palace and take a good look at the creative work of this remarkable architect of the period of classicism.

The second exhibition room is devoted to the contribution of Vasili Stasov to the Catherine Palace. Stasov designed the main study of Alexander I and the adjoining rooms. He also supervised the restoration of the palace after the fire of 1820, carefully and scrupulously reviving the Rastrelli and Cameron rooms, which had suffered badly during the fire.

There is a portrait of Vasili Stasov in the exposition rooms. Furniture and works of applied art of the early 19th century are on display here. Furnishings from the interiors of that time are distinguished by their simple design and precise details. Most of the furniture is made of red wood and Karelian birch. The red-wood chest of drawers is typical, whose smooth polished finish is decorated with bronze brackets shaped like gryphons' heads, small rosettes, and garlands.

In the decoration of the massive French candelabras you can see an ornamental motif common at that time, wreaths, helmets, spears, and shields, reflecting the military spirit of the early 19th century. The accoutrements of the two big candelabras of patinated bronze with sculpture depicting the goddess of victory, Nike, are also symbolic of this prevailing mood.

Clear-cut, harmonious proportion and serene equilibrium are evident in the shape of all these works of decorative applied art, just as in the architecture of classicism.

From the second exhibition room, passing the vaulted and oval inter-communicating rooms you can enter the Main Study of Alexander I, one of the most interesting premises in the palace in its design and artistic decor.

THE MAIN
STUDY OF ALEXANDER I

The Main Study is a rectangular room of particularly austere design and refined architectural forms with a deep semicircular niche separated from the main body of the room by two Ionic columns. Its smooth walls of artificial pale-pink marble are devoid of decoration. The strict composition of the murals on the beams and in the dome of the niche includes motifs of antiquity depicting in particular the different ancient Roman accoutrements and wreaths of laurel leaves. The strict lines and austere colours are softened somewhat by the bronze gilded incrustations used in the decoration of the doors, the window frames, the stove, the mirrors and the furniture.

The furnishings in the main have been completely restored thanks to an extant water-colour by the 19th-century artist Alexei Korzukhin and also from archive data: a large writing-desk under a green table cloth, a walnut armchair with gilded bronze incrustation, and a walnut pedestal cupboard. Motifs of military glory are also used in the artistic design of the furnishings some of which are genuine early 19th-century articles. There is an openwork chandelier designed by Vasili Stasov in the first quarter of the 19th century, decorated with figures of ancient warriors in a chariot; a Russian porcelain vase of 1818 with a depiction of Alexander I's arrival in the suburbs of Paris, in St. Denis on March 14, 1814; the clock on the mantelpiece with the figure of the Roman military leader Julius Caesar. Also of interest in the exposition is a malachite writing set made by Urals craftsmen, the candelabra and the bronze table decorations.

Designed under the supervision of Stasov, the Main Study of Alexander I may be considered an example of an interior of the first quarter of the 19th century in the skill of its execution and its perfection.

The southern part of the suite ends in the Main Study. The next rooms were designed by Cameron to replace Rastrelli's hanging garden.

In spite of the tremendous destruction during the war, some of the elements of their initial architectural finish have been preserved in those rooms, and so their architecture and decor has been completely restored. One of the most interesting rooms created by Cameron is the Green Dining-Room.

THE GREEN DINING-ROOM

Just like the other rooms in the northern part of the palace created by Cameron for the descendent of Catherine the Great, Paul I and his wife Maria Fyodorovna, the Green Dining-Room is built to serve its purpose. Its main attribute is the combination of the refined greenish soft "porcelain-like" hue of the walls with the graceful white moulded decoration which reproduces the murals decorating the villas of Pompeii in volumetric form. In the soft greenish white colour of the room Cameron has boldly introduced a delicate shade of pink into the murals on the door panels and the moulded medallions on the walls.

The moulded decoration in the Green Dining-Room was created by the outstanding Russian sculptor Ivan Martos, the creator of the well-known monument to Kozma Minin and Dmitri Pozharsky in Red Square in Moscow. The sculptor imparted genuinely antique clarity and harmony to scenes about the mythical Poseidon, Phaethon and Hermes. They are executed in high-relief and represent gracefully splendid human figures. The vases, medallions, garlands, and fragments of architecture in low-relief are also imbued with ancient motifs.

The scale and composition of the moulded decoration in the Green Dining-Room is subject to its architectural design to such an extent that it seems that all this has been created in a single upsurge of inspiration by one and the same author.

The room now looks just as it did before the war thanks to surviving fragments, old photographs, and measurements. The Leningrad sculptors E. P. Maslennikov and G. A. Mikhailova have restored the sculptures and most of the moulding on the walls very precisely from old examples; painters have created the murals on the doors from the surviving panels, and the parquet-floor layers have restored the

figured parquet from an old drawing.

Your attention is commanded by the splendid white marble fireplace, with brackets in the form of lions' bodies and irons of gilt bronze, and also by the furniture of the Green Dining-Room: chairs with oval backs and straight legs narrowing towards the floor which were typical of the style of classicism, designed by Cameron, and a writing-desk inlaid with walrus bone worked by bone-carvers from the town of Archangel on the White Sea at the end of the 18th century.

The interior of the Green Dining-Room is a magnificent example of the synthesis of architecture, sculpture, painting, and decorative applied arts, testifying to the brilliant creative fantasy of Cameron based on a profound and subtle understanding of the art of the ancient world. The soft, as it were flowing, architectural forms, the play of volumes, the plasticity of the decoration imparts to Cameron's interiors a special warmth and inspiration.

Compared with the refinement and luxury of the Green Dining-Room, the Waiters' Room next to it is very modest in its decor.

THE WAITERS' ROOM

The main element in the architecture of this room is the symmetrical division of the walls by wooden pilasters painted to look like marble. The fluted pilasters played a purely decorative part, empha-

sizing the austerity of the interior. In the post-war years the pilasters, moulding, doors, figured parquet of rosewood, oak, ebony, and redwood, were restored from surviving fragments. The general colour gamma of the room is pinkish-brown with bright coloured parquet in golden brown hues.

The room has late-18th-century furnishings that were here before 1941. The strict and rectilinear forms of the gaming tables of selected wood and the redwood chairs in classical style are reminiscent of the work of the famous 18th-century English cabinet-maker Thomas Chippendale. His comfortable, solid furniture was popular all over Europe.

The walls of the Waiters' Room are hung with pictures by late 18th-century artists such as "Landscape with Ruins" by Alexei Belski, "Waterfall in Tivoli" by Andrea Locatelli, and "Landscape with a Tower on the Cliff" by an unknown artist.

The Waiters' Room is next to the Blue Drawing-Room, one of the most elegant rooms created by Cameron in the northern part of the palace.

THE BLUE DRAWING-ROOM

The interior of the Blue or Main Drawing-Room is very refined. Soft blue tones, the fine golden patterns of the moulded frieze, the mirror frames and the consoles dominate in its architectural decor.

Using a wide variety of decorative methods—painting and moulding, carving and silk upholstery on the walls and furniture, marbles and mirrors, the architect creates an interior of a single colour composition. The marble caryatids on the fireplace, the ornamental patterns and medallions on the ceiling are in the spirit of antiquity so loved by Cameron.

Destroyed during the war, the Blue Drawing-Room now looks just as it did initially. From the surviving plans the painted ceiling by Cameron with motives from Pompeian frescoes has been restored. The silk fabric was manufactured from an old specimen at a workshop in Moscow.

The parquet floor in the Blue Dining-Room which is composed of different coloured valuable woods has been preserved since the 18th century and may serve as an example of an artistically decorated floor. The extremely complicated technique used in laying the parquet testifies to the great skill of the craftsmen.

In the Drawing-Room you can see part of the big furniture suite and the bronze fireplace decorations designed by Cameron. The chairs and arm-chairs are upholstered with silk and are typical of the elegant gilt furniture of the second half of the 18th century with their clear-cut, precise classical proportions. Rosettes, wreathes, and laurel garlands predominate in their ornamentation.

Cameron is known to have preferred mobile light fittings in designing the lighting for the interiors of Tsarskoye Selo Palace, his candlesticks have not survived. Two magnificent torchères of

Blue Drawing-Room: fireplace grille.

dark-blue glass and crystal with unglazed pottery figures, made at St. Petersburg glass factory at the end of the 18th century, blended well with the furnishings of the Blue Drawing-Room, emphasising its elegance.

The portraits in the Blue Drawing-Room were painted by 18th-century artists. Of special interest is the portrait of Peter the Great by the outstanding Russian painter Ivan Nikitin. Peter, wearing a scarlet cloak over his armour, is depicted by the cannon barrel against the background of a sea battle. In his right hand he holds a staff. The flatness of the background and the sculpture-like body and clothing, the skilful use of light, typical of Nikitin's portraits, intensify the expressiveness of the face and underscore the figure's inner strength. In the portrait of Peter the Great the artist describes a person who is full of energy, courage, firm will and resoluteness, called upon to serve the cause of transforming this country.

In creating a number of vividly realistic works, Nikitin asserted the new stylistic trend in Russian portrait painting which differs from the specific type of portraiture at the end of the 16th and of the 17th centuries which had not yet moved away from icon painting.

The elegant portrait of Catherine I by an unknown artist is interesting. In the manner of execution, this portrait is reminiscent of the work of the French painter Jean Marc Nattier. In counterposition to this magnificent and pompous portrait in the exposition you can see a copy of the portrait of Catherine I by Fyodor Rokotov which is restrained and more intimate in its interpretation of the monarch.

Next to the Blue Drawing-Room there are the small "private rooms" of Maria Fyodorovna, the wife of Paul I; these are the Bed Chamber, the Painting and Sculpture Rooms. Originally designed by Cameron they were rebuilt by Stasov after the fire of 1820.

THE BED CHAMBER

The Bed Chamber which now looks as it did originally is an interesting work of the 18th century in the integrity and expressiveness of its design.

In its interior decor Cameron used faience, bronze, and decorative moulding. Employing antique motifs from the murals in Pompeii as the central piece in the architectural design of the interior, Cameron chose little decorative columns of dazzling white porcelain. Groups of these little columns, light-coloured with thin shafts, garlands of leaves and flowers wound round them, with bases and capitals of gilt bronze, divide off the alcove, serving as support for the light arch decorated with a carved frieze. The multifarious, arabesqued painting on the panels of the eight doors some of which are purely decorative, stand out picturesquely against the background of the columns. Cameron included moulded medallions with allegorical figures of health, cheerfulness, success and sufficiency in the decor, sculptured by Ivan Martos.

The huge windows looking out over the park help to bring nature into the room, imparting a special poetic character to the light-green and blue colour which dominates here.

Among the furnishings of the Bed Chamber you should take a good look at the small dressing table with a hinged top and a mirror. Designed like a trefoil and faced with different types of wood, this unique article of furniture of the second half of the 18th century bears the inscription "the work of the Okhta carpenters, the Naskovs". In the 1720s the Okhta settlement on the Neva was famous for its carpenters and cabinet-makers and later for its mosaic and parquet layers. One of them, the cabinet-maker Naskov, was commissioned to make the dressing table for Maria Fyodorovna (her monogram is inscribed on its top).

The fire grate in the Bed Chamber and the little wrought-iron table were made by famous craftsmen from the town of Tula in burnished steel with gilt bronze. The dark-blue glass table was designed by Cameron, the sculpture of cupid in the niche was designed by Nicolas-François Gillet.

Next to the Bed Chamber there are the **Painting** and **Sculpture Rooms**. In these tiny rooms elements of Cameron's initial interiors have partly been preserved, but motifs characteristic of the art of the beginning of the 19th century predominate. The murals and moulding of the ceiling were designed by Vasili Stasov. The private chambers are situated in the Small Suite like the rest of the living quarters in the palace.

After you have seen the Bed Chamber, you should return to the Main Suite to go to the Chinese Blue Drawing-Room.

Gates to the palace's courtyard.

Catherine Palace: a view from the French garden.

The palace is always full of visitors.

Main Staircase.

Great Hall. It took experts several decades to restore the palace.

State Dining-Room. Pieces of the hunters' china dinner service and a vase on a gilded console table (left).

Portrait Gallery: the plafond allegorically depicting the gods of Olympus.

Amber Room: fragment of parquet floor; amber chests.

Picture Gallery: carved gilded portal.

Picture Gallery: general view.

Tile from a stove by Russian masters, 18th century.

Main Study of Alexander I.

Green Dining-Room: fragments of interior and moulded decoration.

Studio (left) and Blue Dining-Room (right).

Bed Chamber (left).

*Chinese Blue Drawing-Room:
fireplace and fragment of silk
upholstery on walls.*

Antechoir.

*Catherine Park: general view
of the central avenue in the
Old Garden.*

*Landscape Park. Evening
Hall. Marble Bridge.
Alexander Park.*

*Cameron Gallery: view from
the Great Pond.*

THE CHINESE
BLUE DRAWING-ROOM

In the 18th century the exotic "Chinese style" manifested itself in European art, and Chinese motifs appeared in architecture and ornamentation.Chinese laquered objets d'art, delicate porcelain, vases, and all kinds of graceful knickknacks were in high regard. But particularly widespread in Europe were the beautifully embroidered or painted Chinese silk fabrics. The drawing-room created by Cameron got its name from them. Its walls were covered with Chinese blue silk with fantastic landscapes and genre scences in different coloured Indian ink.

Paying tribute to the fashion of the time, Cameron did, however, know how to combine this wall decoration with elements of ornamentation in antique spirit in a talented manner. The moulded gilt frieze, the fireplace, the painted ceiling depicting personages from ancient mythology, and the paintings on the doors are all in the style of classicism.

After the war the Leningrad artist and restorer R. D. Slepushkina painted the silk specially made for the Chinese Blue Drawing-Room from surviving specimens and pre-war photographs. The ceiling was repainted from Cameron's sketches. The paintings on the doors, the fireplace, the graceful carved console with the mirror above it, and the magnificent parquet of ebony, redwood, rosewood, sandal wood and maple have all been restored. The suite of gilt furniture upholstered with blue silk dating from the end of the 18th century, the table with the mosaic top and the Chinese porcelain vases are in good harmony with the bright colours of the drawing-room's walls. Completing the interior is a portrait of the Empress Elizabeth, who is depicted by the 18th-century artist Johannes Groot as the goddess of flowers, Flora, and a gouache by the eminent Russian painter Semyon Shchedrin "A View of the Imatru Waterfall".

Between the Chinese Blue Drawing-Room and the choir of the palace church there is the so-called antechoir.

THE ANTECHOIR

Just like the Chinese Blue Drawing-Room the decor of the Antechoir is predominated by the bright colourful silk covering on the walls, but this time of a golden colour. These silk wall hangings, Russian work of the second half of the 18th century with depictions of peacocks, pheasants and other birds, were preserved in evacuation and are a unique artistic treasure. They were woven on handlooms by Russian serf weavers at the factory of the merchant Lazarev in the village of Fryanovo near Moscow, designed by the artist and weaver

Antechoir: fragment of decor.

from Lyons Philippe de Lassalle. In the 19th century, similar fabric was manufactured at other mills in Russia from these specimens. The factory-made fabrics of the 19th century can be seen in the upholstery of the gilt furniture suite and in the curtains of the Antechoir which have been preserved in their original form thanks to the evacuation.

At the present time, the Antechoir looks just as it did originally. The restored elements of its architecture combined with the elegant festive wall paper and furniture impart individuality to the room's interior decor.

The doors of the Antechoir lead to the last premises in the Main Suite, the Choir of the Palace Church.

THE CHOIR OF THE PALACE CHURCH

The tsar's pew, a large choir divided by a partition from the nave, was on the first floor. The members of the royal family would sit here during services. The architecture of the choir, like that of the church itself is characteristic of the baroque style and was designed by Rastrelli.

A narrow stone staircase joins the choir to the church.

THE CATHERINE PALACE CHURCH

In its colourfulness and the expressiveness of its design the spacious body of the church lit by windows on both sides was one of Rastrelli's most typical interiors.

Like the Main Suite, the church was

elegant: the white Corinthian columns wound about with carved garlands, golden figures of angels, sculptured groups and ornamental details stood out against the background of the walls painted with Berlin varnish.

The bright, festive colours of the paintings, icons in gilt figure frames, painted panels and paintings on the ceiling corresponded to the architecture. The best painters and court carvers helped to create the iconostasis, which forms a solid wall from floor to ceiling. The ceiling was painted by the artist Giuseppe Valeriani.

During the War against Nazism the church was subjected to barbarous destruction. The Nazis demolished the iconostasis, plundered 96 icons, destroyed the painted plafond and the architectural ornamentation.

At the moment, only conservation work is being conducted in the church. In the future all the elements of its decor will be completely restored according to Rastrelli's design. Between the church and the vestibule on the ground floor there is a spacious, practically designed premises, the church antechamber erected by Vasili Stasov in the 1840s.

THE CHURCH ANTECHAMBER

In its architectural decoration you are aware of Stasov's striving to use Rastrelli's compositional methods to unite it stylistically with the interior of the church. The capitals of the columns, the carved decorations on the doors, the wall panels and the ceiling are in the Rococo style. In its gamma of colours a combination of white and gold predominates, making the room elegant and festive.

A visit to the church antechamber which was restored after the war completes your tour of the Catherine Palace, this remarkable monument of Russian artistic culture of the 18th century which has been reborn after the Second World War.

THE CATHERINE PARK

The Catherine Palace is the compositional centre of a big architectural and park ensemble. The Catherine Park is an inseparable and extremely poetic part of the ensemble. It is a magnificent work of creative labour by several generations of talented Russian architects, sculptors, gardeners, engineers and thousands of craftsmen and working people of various specializations.

The magnificent avenues of the old park are crowded with people both in summer and in winter. Not only Leningraders come here but also tourists

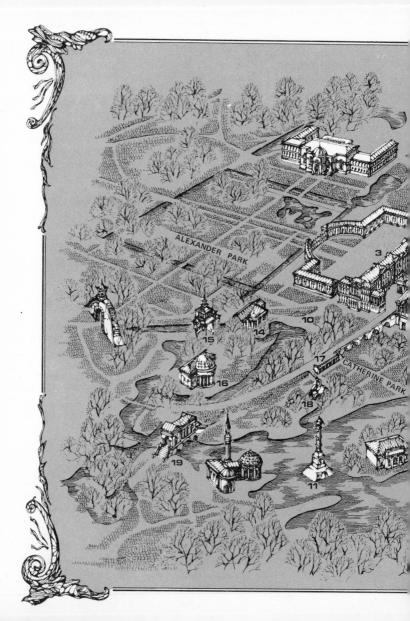

ALEXANDER PARK

CATHERINE PARK

3

10

14

15

16

17

18

19

11

Great
Pond

CATHERINE PARK

1. Monument to Pushkin in the Lyceum Garden
2. Lyceum
3. Catherine Palace
4. Upper Bath
5. Lower Bath
6. Hermitage
7. Grotto
8. Admiralty
9. Cameron Gallery. Agate Rooms
10. Kagul Obelisk
11. Cheshme Column
12. Morea Column
13. "My Kind Colleagues" Gates
14. Evening Hall
15. Creaking Chinese Summer House
16. Concert Hall
17. Granite Terrace
18. "Milkmaid" Fountain
19. Marble Bridge

from all over the Soviet Union and from abroad.

To take a look at the symmetrical and landscape parks, the most interesting monuments, and the park sculptures, it is best to enter the park through the gate by the "**Swan**" **Fountain**. You begin your walk near the main entrance of the Catherine Palace on the terrace of the Old Garden (now part of the park) which was laid out at the beginning of the 18th century during the reign of Catherine I.

At the time, French gardens were popular in Russia. The basis of this composition was the idea of the exact symmetry of the areas around the palace which was the main element in the ensemble, a strict system of individual pavilions and structures. Embellished with straight, geometrically divided rows of trees trimmed in the form of balls and cubes, and the whimsical patterns of the parterres, the French garden corresponded completely to the current aesthetic ideals of the first half of the 18th century which were engendered in France in the 17th century.

However, in their artistic design the Russian parks of that time were rather original owing to national traditions and natural conditions and, most important, the local species of trees such as firs, birches, and junipers, which replaced the European boxtrees in the parks.

The simple lawn was considered a splendid decorative element in the cold climate. Its green carpet combined with the slender rows of trees imparted an elegant, monumental nature to Russian park compositions.

In the Catherine Park you can see original features of landscape gardening art characteristic of a Russian estate at the end of the 17th century: the palace, the centre of the ensemble, picturesquely located on a natural hill as if on a pedestal, or the structures skilfully interwoven with the landscape, clumps of lime-trees which are resistant to the northern frosts, the moist soil and the damp climate prevailing. The lawn of the Old Garden laid out on the slopes of the gradually descending earthen terraces and in geometrically-shaped glades were almost the main decorative element in the park composition of the Old Garden.

All these peculiarities of the Russian garden and park style you can see in the elegant part of the Catherine park recreated in the post-war years from the surviving drawings and notes of Kvasov, Chevakinsky, and Rastrelli.

The symmetrical composition of the Catherine Park occupying an area of 102 hectares between the palace and the cascade ponds produces an austere and solemn impression. The slender rows of the live colonnade of tree trunks disappear into the distance. Paths branch out as radii. The central avenue of the Old Garden is the main compositional axis of the ensemble, connecting the palace with the Hermitage.

From the upper terrace you can easily discern the division of the park into two parts, the lower plain part, and the upper (in front of the palace) part which descends in terraces joined by stone staircases.

On the terrace stretching along the façade of the palace your attention is commanded by the fancifully arranged **Parterre**, reminiscent of the patterns on the parquet floors of the palace halls. The so-called "embroidered parterres" are a unique mosaic of broken bricks, coal, ground glass, and sand of various shades and were a favourite embellishment of symmetrical parks in the 18th century. A hedge of small lime bushes, which always figured in these parks, has been recreated in the symmetrical, old park of the Catherine Park. Crisscrossed by avenues lined with ornamentally clipped trees and patterned parterres, the Old Garden emphasized the solemnity and festiveness of the palace and did as it were serve as a continuation of its elegant rooms.

For more than two centuries marble statues of the heroes of ancient Greek and Roman mythology embellished the symmetrical part of the Catherine Park, standing out picturesquely amidst the green of the trees and lawns.

THE MARBLE SCULPTURES

The numerous marble sculptures in the Catherine Park were created by masters of the Venetian school—Pietro Baratta, Giovanni Bonazza, Antonio Tarsia, Giovanni Zarzoni—specially for Peter the Great who supervised the purchase of them himself. He believed that in St. Petersburg, the new capital of Russia, plastic art was called upon to assist in disseminating the ideas of the time. The depictions of antique gods and heroes were not only meant to embellish the gardens in the capital but were also to instill in the viewer the spirit of desire for courageous deeds.

Moreover, the French gardens offered the masters of decorative art boundless scope. By their arrangement against the background of copses or semicircular niches of clipped greenery, forming as it were a single structure corresponding to the outline of the given area, the marble statues created an original spatial rhythm in the layout of the garden.

In the mid-18th century, on the orders of Empress Elizabeth, sixty more statues, mostly on mythological subjects, were brought from the Summer Garden in St. Petersburg, the scene of court amusements and festivities. Individual allegorical figures were "Gloria", "Love for Motherland", "Peace" and others, which personified the prosperity of the country during the rule of Peter the Great, love for homeland, and military power. The garden in Tsarskoye Selo, once embellished with statues and sculptured groups became a kind of museum of sculpture in the style of late baroque. The sculptured depictions of gods and heroes were mainly decorative, exhibiting the fanciful refinement and dynamism of forms. The original

*Decorative sculptures in the
portico at the palace entrance.*

pathetic element is combined in them with a lightness, gracefulness, and elegant poses, expressiveness of the silhouette, and skilful free composition in communicating movement.

At the very entrance to the palace, in a portico there are four sculptures— "Love for Motherland", "Sybil of Libya", "Iola", and "Sophia (Wisdom) Trampling on Vice". On the park's upper terrace, right next to the palace, the statues "Peace" and "Magnificence" have been erected symmetrically. Along the arrow-straight Hermitage Avenue, which runs from the palace's main entrance across the park to one of the best park pavilions, the Hermitage, statues have also been erected symmetrically in pairs: "Perseus" (to the left of the entrance) and "Andromeda" (to the right of the entrance), "Poro" and "Spring", "Galatea" and "Amphitrite", "Heracles" and "Military Valour". The statue of Galatea, a young sea nymph astride a dolphin with a scarf waving above her head, is conspicuous for its special grace. The statue of Amphitrite, the wife of the sea god Poseidon, is equally graceful.

Also imposing and expressive are the statues of "Peace", a fine young woman with a torch held down, "Love for the Homeland", depicted as a warrior trampling on enemy arms and "Military Valour", an Amazon in armour and a helmet with luxurious plumes, holding a shield on which there is an eagle fighting a lion, the symbol of Russia defeating its foes. The statue of Heracles is as it were reminiscent of Peter the Great and the victorious end of the Great Northern War against the Swedes, as a result of which Russia regained her access to the Baltic Sea.

The masters of garden sculpture at the beginning of the 18th century not only strove to find the most beneficial positions for their statues sometimes uniting them into groups to tell a story in the language of plastic. Thus in the French garden of the Catherine Park busts symbolizing the changes in the seasons of the year, the months of March, April, May and June, have been set up. Created by the Italian sculptor Giovanni Bonazza they are distinguished for their careful details and the rich effect of light and shade. The decorativeness and picturesque location of the statues against the background of the greenery and the lawns imparts a charm and finish to the artistic look of the French park, the white marble emphasizing its elegance.

To the left of the Hermitage Avenue, on the side of the Mirror Pond, there is the pavilion, The Upper Bath.

THE UPPER BATH

The pavilion the Upper Bath or "The Bath-Houses of Their Highnesses" which is austere in its design was erected by the architect Ilya Neyelov in 1777-1779, completes the view of the pond. The building is rectangular in shape with a three-edged projection above the entrance; its façade, almost completely devoid of ornamentation, with a light-moulded garland above the door is typical of the architecture of early classicism. Designed in the classical forms novel to that period, thanks to its well-founded proportions it merged well into the landscape of the symmetrical park. Its pale yellow walls crowned with a parapet stand out clearly against the trees, picturesquely reflected in the mirror-like surface of the pond.

In contradistinction to the modest outer façades of the pavilion its interior decor is extremely elegant. Motifs from the murals in the so-called "Golden House of Nero" discovered during excavations in Rome are used in its decor. The central octagonal room, intended for recreation, was decorated by Alexei Belsky copying Italian engravings; today it had been restored from sketches under the supervision of the artist A. V. Treskin. This festive and elegant interior is embellished by a plafond and two painted panels above the doors depicting scenes from the myth about Phaethon, the son of the Sun God, and also decorative painting consisting of garlands of flowers and fruits.

Now the pavilion houses a reading room in summertime.

Parallel to the Upper Bath on the lower terrace of the Catherine Park there is the pavilion of the Lower Bath, or the "Cavaliers' Bath-House" built by Ilya Neyelov in 1779. It served as a bath-house for the courtiers in the eighteenth century.

THE LOWER BATH

In this pavilion six round chambers and four rectangular rooms are grouped around the main round hall. Warm water was supplied to the big copper bath in the hall by pipes from two water-heaters. The rest rooms have marble fireplaces.

The external appearance of the building has remained unchanged, its walls, devoid of decoration, cut by small round lights.

From the Lower Bath you can go down the central avenue of the Old Garden to one of the most interesting monuments in the Catherine Park, the Hermitage, which is quite rightly regarded as a work of art of Russian garden and park architecture.

THE HERMITAGE

Simultaneously with the Catherine Palace, the eminent architects Mikhail Zemtsov, Alexei Kvasov, Savva Chevakinsky and Bartolomeo Rastrelli were erecting the Hermitage (from 1744 to 1756) on an artificial islet formed by a

PARK SCULPTURES

fairly deep moat and faced with black and white marble slabs.

The building's location at the end of the main (Hermitage) avenue leading from the palace, the rich ornamentation on the façades—glittering gilded statues, garlands, masks, shells, magnificent window casings, the dazzling whiteness of the 64 Corinthian columns and the bright azure colour of the walls—all created the impression of elegance and festiveness and made the Hermitage part of the palace.

The pavilion is octagonal-shaped with four extensions built onto the sides and a balustrade running round the edge of the roof. At one time, statues were mounted on the balustrade and between the groups of columns. The central cupola was crowned with a gilded sculptured group "The Rape of Proserpina", cupids and carved garlands. These sculptures were plundered and destroyed by the Nazis during the war. In spite of all these losses, extremely rare examples of the decorative sculpture of the mid-eighteenth century are to be found in the carved ornamentation on the façades of the pavilion. These are the extraordinarily precisely executed stucco bas-reliefs in the niches of the bases of the columns, the cartouches and lion masks, with their rich, pronounced sculptured features, and the tracery of the balcony grilles.

In the richness and variety of their decor the interiors of the Hermitage were on a par with that of the best rooms in the palace. The decor of the pavilion's main hall particularly evoked the admiration of contemporaries. The big windows, the numerous mirrors, the illusory painting on the plafond did, as it were, extend the dimensions of the room, linking the interior with the park around the pavilion. The fanciful patterns on the light wooden gilded carving are repeated over and over again, being reflected in the mirrors.

The magnificent plafond was decorated by Giuseppe Valeriani, in accordance with the purpose of the room to entertain and amuse the owner of the estate and his or her close friends. It depicts the gods feasting on Mount Olympus and Juno and Jupiter invite the inhabitants of the heavens to take their places at the feast. The decoration on the plafond creates the illusion that the hall has an upper tier. The traditional elements of decoration—the fluffy clouds and the figures of hovering geniuses—were not only significant in themselves, but also imparted a lightness and airiness to the whole composition.

Valeriani's picturesque panels above the mirrors stand out for their bright colours. They depict scenes from Ovid's *Metamorphoses*: "Bacchus and Ariadne", "Apollo Pursuing Daphne", "The Rape of Europa", "Bacchus Crowning Ariadne with a Crown of Seven Stars".

The Hermitage was not only famous for its splendid, refined design, for which it was considered one of the major sights of Tsarskoye Selo. Guests, who had the honour of visiting the imperial summer residence, were astounded at all the different kinds of complicated devices installed here. There was no staircase leading from the ground to the first floors. Guests ascended in special armchairs. The tables laid for 35 people were also lifted to the upper floor by special mechanisms through an aperture in the ceiling; at the end of the meal, the tables were lowered again, and the dining hall became a ballroom.

Restoration work is at present being completed on the Hermitage which was badly damaged during the war. It will not be long before this wonderful monument embodying the great achievements of Russian and world architecture of the eighteenth century, a synthesis of architecture, painting and sculpture, will be open to the public.

THE GROTTO

Of the other structures created by Bartolomeo Rastrelli that have survived in the Catherine Palace there is the Grotto, an original pavilion with a fanciful high roof, effectively located on the northern side of the Great Pond not far from the Hermitage. Intended as a nook for a rest on the hot summer days, pavilions of this type were an inseparable part of the landscape of the symmetrical garden. The Grotto is an important element in the Catherine Park ensemble. Typical of late baroque, the façades of the building are embellished with rusticated columns, doors with intricately carved frames, and windows with ornate carvings. A graceful pattern adorns the balustrade running round the edge of the roof. At one time wooden sculptures helped to break up its monotonous rhythm.

The pavilion gets its name from the moulded decorations on its façades and interior devoted to marine subjects. Dolphins' heads are depicted on the capitals of the columns, and masks of Neptune on the keystones above the windows. The domed pedestal of the fountain is decorated with sea deities pouring water from vessels, and complicated wavy shells and the heads of sea monsters bedeck the high roof of the building.

The open-work wrought-iron and copper leaf grilles on the windows and doors reminiscent of lace, complete the ornamentation on the outside of the pavilion. These are among the best examples of eighteenth-century Russian metal work.

Rastrelli's plan to decorate the premises with different coloured sea shells and porous tuff was not carried out. The extant interior decor of the Grotto, light graceful moulding on the walls, was designed by Antonio Rinaldi.

Today the Grotto is used as an exhibition pavilion.

From the little ornamented square on the shore where the Grotto stands, you get a view of the Great Pond, one of the most beautiful man-made pools in the Catherine Park.

Sculptures of ancient philosophers, scholars and poets on the open terraces of the Cameron Gallery.

Gates by the Cold Bath (the Agate Rooms).

Morea Column.

Lower Bath.

*Chinese or Creaking Summer
House.*

*Cheshme Column dedicated to
the Russian naval victory over
the Turks in 1770.*

Grotto.

"Milkmaid" Fountain.

THE PONDS, POOLS,
AND CANALS

Of great decorative importance in laying out symmetrical parks were the artificial water bodies such as ponds, canals, and pools with motionless surfaces that would reflect the architecture of structures on their banks. There were no large expanses of water in Tsarskoye Selo. Since the locality was relatively high up, it had no rivers and lakes except for the little river Vangasi. Therefore, the lack of running water made itself felt right from the beginning of the construction work.

In the beginning, when the royal family was in residence at Tsarskoye Selo, water was brought from St. Petersburg in vats. In 1749, a gravity flow aqueduct was built in wooden pipes from the Vittolovsky Springs, approximately four kilometres from Pushkin; in 1773, when that aqueduct could no longer satisfy all the needs in water, the construction of the 16-kilometre-long Taitsky aqueduct was started which it took 14 years to build. In 1787, this hydro-engineering installation, which was unique in its design for that time, began to supply running water to the man-made water bodies in the Tsarskoye Selo parks.

By this time the Great and Cascade (or Lower) Ponds had been deepened considerably and their banks were lined with a hexagonal frame.

At the present time, the water surfaces in the Pushkin parks occupy an area of 342,000 square metres, and the volume of water in the running water bodies is 325,000 cubic metres. The area of the park's main pool, the **Great Pond**, is approximately 16 hectares. The banks of the pond, which was constructed right at the beginning of the eighteenth century on the site of a stream, were gradually improved and their shape changed. New pavilions richly ornamented with sculptures and gilding and other structures were erected around it and carefully selected trees were planted.

The dissected banks of the Great Pond, forming peninsulas and little bays with silver willows leaning over the water, the hues of the foliage of maples, aspens, limes and oaks continuously changing in the sun's rays, the wide sparkling surface of the water and the façades of the buildings contrasting with the green background allow us to consider the Great Pond and its banks one of the most picturesque spots in the park.

With the help of a dam erected by its east bank, the Great Pond supplies the **Cascade** or **Lower Ponds**. With its weirs, tall decorative trees, and fantastic heaps of rock fragments and stones, they are very beautiful even today. A tall hill made from the soil dug out when constructing the ponds appeared near one of the Cascade Ponds in the 1770s. It was called Trifon Hill after the gardener Trifon Ilyin.

The banks of the picturesque canals

laid across the park in the eighteenth century are connected by more than twenty bridges and dams. The **Fish Canal**, which formed the boundary of the Old Garden in the eighteenth century, stretched parallel to the Catherine Palace at the end of the Hermitage Avenue. The canal is spanned by humpbacked bridges erected in the 1770s and designed by the architect Vasili Neyelov. It is thought that fish were bred in this canal for the tsar's table, and therefore it was called "Rybny" meaning "Fish" Canal.

Time has not spared the numerous hydro-engineering installations but those that have survived have lost none of their picturesqueness, and even now they remain "the very spirit of the landscape", its main ornament.

THE ADMIRALTY

On the south side of the Great Pond your attention will be attracted by a grouping of three red-brick pavilions. Their original silhouette, their crenellated towers and the tiered pediment of the main building look very pretty against the lush greenery of the park. Vasili Neyelov used motifs of Gothic architecture, which were common in park structures in the second half of the eighteenth century. The ensemble was called the "Admiralty" because the premises on the ground floor were used for storing the sailing and rowing boats of the Tsarskoye Selo "Flotilla"; on the first floor of the main pavilion there was the so-called Dutch rest room.

The buildings at the sides, shaped like round towers, housed swans, pheasants and peacocks, which were bred here for the ponds in the park.

At the present time, the façades of the pavilions are being restored, and there is now a restaurant in one of them.

THE CAMERON ENSEMBLE

This light, but at the same time monumental structure designed by Charles Cameron, was beautifully described by Alexander Pushkin:

There in silence the lofty mansions,
Leaning on their vaults, rush upwards to the clouds.

("Reminiscences in Tsarskoye Selo", 1814).

Charles Cameron, the talented architect who was fanatically keen on the ancient world, came to Russia from England in the summer of 1779. That was the time when Russia's prestige was being boosted considerably by military victories and its standing among the major world powers was enhanced. Its ties with Europe, with European culture facilitated the dissemination in the advanced circles of Russian society of the progressive ideas of the Enlightenment

A view of the Cameron Baths.

Stone mask on an arch.

and had an impact on the formation of the aesthetic principles of classicism.

In architecture the new style was manifest in the absence of luxurious decoration. The "exultant" architecture of the middle of the century with its excessively ornate designs, broken fanciful forms, dynamic nature, picturesqueness and abundance of moulded and carved gilt patterns, was replaced by more serene, better balanced and austere forms. In these edifices, solemnity and elegance was attained by the classical precision of the proportions, the linear rhythm, and accentuation of the part played by the order in its antique form.

In spite of this passion for the beauty of Antiquity, however, the buildings the architect created in the style of early classicism were imbued with genuinely

Russian national originality, continuing the traditions of ancient Russian architecture. According to the figurative words of the famous art critic Yevgeni Lanceré, one of the scholars of the works of Charles Cameron, "western art on Russian soil, in a Russian climate, in Russian conditions has become something close in its spirit to us, something really Russian ..."

Cameron worked at Tsarskoye Selo from 1779 until 1795. Over that period he created one of his biggest structures, which came to be known as the Cameron Baths. This was the Cold Bath-House, the hanging garden and the gallery, in which he employed elements of the architecture of monumental Ancient Roman public baths or "thermae".

Cameron's baths are perceived well from different sides. But a particularly striking impression is created by the light Cameron Gallery, which seems to be floating in the air, if you approach it

*Exhibition of Costumes and
Decorative and Applied Art of
the 18th- early
20th Centuries.*

monumental socle faced with grey stone. The impression of amazing lightness is created by the fact that the columns are placed far apart and linked together at the bottom by an open-work grille; also by the contrast between the upper and lower stories, between the primitive, somewhat rough masonry of the walls, the sturdily built arcade, which look as if the rustication and the capitals of the ground floor have been worn away by time, and the more carefully worked forms and lines of the architectural order of the gallery.

A large main staircase, divided into two arc-like staircases in its upper part, leads up to the colonnade. Here the eye is caught by the heavy grey stone steps of the lower part and the gracefully curved flights of stairs and the open-work banisters of the upper part. The piers of the staircase serve as the pedestals for two huge bronze statues—"Heracles" and "Flora", cast in 1786 from antique originals by the sculptor Fyodor Gordeyev and the well-known founder Vasili Mozhalov.

In the middle of the gallery there is a glazed hall for strolls in bad weather. Bronze busts of ancient philosophers, scholars, poets, statesmen, and military leaders, copies of antique originals, which are kept in the State Hermitage today, stood between the columns on the open terraces. Noteworthy is the bronze bust of Mikhail Lomonosov by a contemporary and friend, Fyodor Shubin.

From the terraces a splendid view of the Great Pond, the Grotto and Admi-

from the Great Pond side. Its snow-white, irreproachably slender columns, standing high above the park, contrast effectively with the dark-green of the trees, and definitely show up whiter in the twilight after sunset.

Cameron built the gallery in exceptionally bold design. He erected a light, slender Ionic colonnade mounted on a

ralty pavilions opens out framed by clumps of trees on its banks, the park stretching away into the distance with its glades and fancifully winding alleys and paths, and the boundless sky above this wonderful landscape.

From the gallery visitors enter the Hanging Garden, an open veranda on arches, raised to the level of the first floor. The garden is fitted with lead flooring covered with a fairly thick layer of soil so that shrubs and trees can be grown there.

The southern façade of the Agate Rooms abuts upon the Hanging Garden. The entrance to them is a rotonda-like portico with columns and a small dome.

THE AGATE ROOMS

The focal point of the Cameron ensemble is the pavilion of the Cold Baths or the Agate Rooms. The architect's passion for Roman thermae, to the study of which he devoted more than twenty years of his life, is most evident here in the composition of the Baths, its exterior, planning and the exquisite taste and fine perception of the interior decor.

The ground floor of the building housed the Cold Baths, a room with a large tin swimming pool, and the hot baths, a warm room with warm water. The rooms for rest were on the upper floor.

The motifs of ancient Rome predominate in the interior decor here. However, in drawing upon the methods of decoration from the arsenal of ancient Roman architects, Cameron attempted not just to make a copy of an antique building, but artistically revealed the functional significance of the premises, which also determine their decor. The decoration on the ground floor is mostly moulded. The sculptor, Jean-Dominique Rachette embellished the

vaults, the arches and walls of the frigidarium, the room with the swimming pool, with exquisitely drawn medallions, sculptured friezes, and panels depicting numerous figures in antique scenes.

Cameron's unprecedented skill as a decorator made itself felt in the interior decor of the rooms on the first floor. In the richness of their furnishings these rooms are on a par with the main rooms in the palace. The decoration in the Jasper and Agate Rooms situated on both sides of the central main hall, are a real collection of precious stones from the Urals and the Altai.

Delivered to St. Petersburg in the 1750s, it was not until twenty years later that a use was found for the jasper, agate, and crystal in Cameron's interiors. The sheets of green jasper were used to face the panels for the Jasper Chamber, and the dark red agate called "meat agate" in the eighteenth century, for the Agate Room. This is why the Cameron pavilion came to be known as the Agate Rooms.

The main hall of the Agate Rooms

which served as a place for amusement, games and feasts, is reminiscent in its architecture of one of the rooms in the thermae of Diocletian, a Roman emperor of the end of the third and the beginning of the fourth centuries. The matt gloss of its walls covered with artificial marble of a delicate peach colour, the greyish pink Olonetz marble of the eight Corinthian columns, the whiteness of the marble of the torches in the form of antique female figures holding gilt lamps, and the vases of jasper and porphyry mounted in the niches create a noble gamma of colours. It is enhanced by the redwood and rosewood door panels, the multifarious pattern of the decorative parquet designed by Yu. Felten for one of the palaces in St. Petersburg.

The exterior of the Agate Rooms is exceptionally fine in its graceful simplicity and the precise proportions. The massive socle faced with grey stone and designed with deliberately archaic details, links the building with the Cameron Gallery, imparting unity to the architectural style of the entire thermae complex.

The semicircular terra-cotta niches typical of Pompeii with the dark bronze statues and the high rectangular "French" balconies with graceful railings contrast sharply with the pale-ochre plastered walls of the first floor. Giving his due to the beauty of the smooth wall, Cameron does not divide it up by profiles or pilasters but enlivens solely with round bas-reliefs, using his favourite motif, moulded medallions on mythological subjects.

On the Hanging Gardens side, Cameron inserts a light colonnade into the main façade of the Agate Rooms on the first floor. This oval semi-rotonda unites the Cold Baths stylistically with the Cameron Gallery, emphasizing the unity of the structures.

When in the Agate Rooms, which are open to visitors in summer, you can go into the park down a specially constructed gently sloping ramp. The design and ornamentation of this decorative structure, reminiscent of the ruins of ancient Rome, are also imbued with the spirit of Antiquity. The arched vaults, the mighty Doric semi-columns supporting the descending path, the giant masks of the gods and heroes of ancient mythology on the keystones of the seven arches impart solemnity and picturesqueness to the structure.

Just like the massive socle of the Agate Rooms and the ground floor of the Cameron Gallery, the ramp is built of Pudozh stone. This choice of material was not accidental for its colour and rough surface reminded the architect of the weather-beaten stones of the architectural monuments of Antiquity. The ramp leads straight from the Cameron buildings into the landscape park, as it were, forming the beginning of the so-called Ramp Avenue.

The famous Cameron thermae are a unique architectural ensemble in which the architect manifested a profoundly individual, creative interpretation of Antiquity through the prism of his own epoch. Today, 200 years later, Cameron's splendid buildings are just as bright and beautiful, an inseparable part of the poetic landscapes, quite rightly referred to as the "Graeco-Roman rhapsody" of the Catherine Park.

From the ramp you get a good view of the magnificent marble Cheshme Rostral Column towering in the centre of the Great Pond. This is one of several monuments in the Catherine Park devoted to the brilliant victories of the Russian forces in the war with Turkey in 1768-1774.

THE MILITARY GLORY MONUMENTS

The magnificent monuments designed by Antonio Rinaldi and erected in the Catherine Park in the 1700s are distinguished by the refined form characteristic of early classicism, precision of silhouette, fine proportions and their skilfully chosen location in the park. Built of Russian marbles of wide variety of colours, they also testify to the interest taken in Russia at that time in materials which lent themselves splendidly to decorative sculpture. In contrast to the bright polychromy of baroque, the use of the colours offered by Russian marble, a stone of serene, refined tones, imparted a uniqueness both to individual elements of the monuments as well as to the general composition of the edifices typical of early classicism.

THE CHESHME COLUMN

The twenty-metre high rostral column erected in 1774-1778 appears to rise out of the water of the Great Pond. The column was erected at the same time as the line of the pond's sides was altered to give it the outline of Cheshme Bay in the Aegean Sea, where the famous sea battle between the Russians and the Turks was waged on the night of June 25-26 (Julian Calendar), 1770. In that battle, the Russian sailors commanded by Admiral Georgi Sviridov destroyed the Turkish fleet, which had until that time been considered invincible. "On the night of the 25th and 26th the enemy, the Turkish navy fleet, was attacked, defeated, smashed to smithereens, burned, blown up, sent to the bottom, and turned to ashes," wrote the admiral in his report.

The brilliant victory in Cheshme Bay determined the outcome of the war in Russia's favour. It evoked a great upsurge of patriotic sentiment and became the subject of many works of art.

The Cheshme Column is composed of different varieties of marble: the shaft is embellished with symmetrically placed rostra of pale pink marble, the pedestal is of grey marble, and the base of red stone. The column stands on a pyramidal base, faced with grey granite, which is immersed in the water.

The refined gamma of marbles in the Cheshme Column, its dark bronze ornamentation, the six rostra, in whose composition all the possible military accoutrements are included, are in splendid harmony with the sparkling clear waters of the Great Pond and with the picturesque domes of the trees framing its banks.

The column is topped by an allegorical sculpture by I. Schwarz, a bronze eagle pecking away at the half moon, the symbol of the East. The sculpture symbolises Russia's victory over Turkey. The pedestal of the column bears three bronze bas-reliefs depicting the major sea battles of the Russo-Turkish war.

During their temporary occupation of Pushkin the Nazis tried in vain to pull down the Cheshme Column with a rope tied to a tank. Then they stripped off two of the bas-reliefs and smelted them down. The third bas-relief was found badly damaged in a copper foundry not far from the station of Antropshino near Leningrad.

In the post-war years the architect A. Kedrinsky and a team of restorers by using graphic and archive materials have managed to make the monument look as it did originally. Later on, the lost bronze plaques from the pedestal will be restored.

THE KAGUL OBELISK

Right next to the Cameron Gallery and to its ramp there is the Kagul Obelisk, erected in memory of the defeat of the multitudinous Turkish army on the river Kagul by the forces of the Russian military leader Pyotr Rumyantsev. The inscription on the pedestal of the obelisk reads: "...on July 21st, 1770, under the command of Count Pyotr Rumyantsev, the Russian army seventeen thousand strong, put to flight to the river Danube the Turkish Vizier Halil-Bei with a force of 150,000 men".

The light, slender four-sided marble monument, simple in silhouette, stands not far from the palace, in the so-called "Private Garden", which was laid out on this spot later on. From the obelisk you get a splendid view of the broad green meadow descending the hillside and the picturesque smooth surfaces of the upper ponds and canals.

There are no military accoutrements in the ornamentation of the Kagul Obelisk. The beauty of its silhouette, its refined exquisite proportions and also the skilfully chosen dark-grey and red Russian marble, harmonising well with the greenery of the park in summer and with the white snows in winter make it austerely magnificent.

Nestling in a clump of trees not far from the Kagul Obelisk you can see a massive, tall **Rectangle** of grey mottled pink marble standing on a three-tiered granite base. The bronze plaque attached to one side of the base reads: "How great is the pleasure experienced by honest souls when they see the good deeds and merits deservedly rewarded with the praise of all." Above the plaque there is a gilded coat of arms belonging to Catherine the Great's favourite, Alexander Lanskoy, and below the inscription are the two sides of a memorial medal. The monument is crowned with a white marble urn, which looks like a tongue of flame at the top.

The originality of the choice of colour, the hue and texture of the material, the well-balanced proportions and graceful outline of the elements allow it to be assumed that the monument to Alexander Lanskoy, like the other monuments commemorating feats of arms in the Catherine Park, was designed by Antonio Rinaldi.

THE "FOR MY KINDLY COLLEAGUES" GATES

On the south-eastern fringe of the Catherine Park by the road along which the Russian forces returned from their campaign after the victory over Napoleon, the gates "For My Kindly Colleagues" were erected by Vasili Stasov, who had upheld the tradition of erecting monuments commemorating feats of arms in the Catherine Park in the first quarter of the nineteenth century. The monumental cast-iron portico with two rows of sturdy columns in the austere, simple, laconic forms typical of Stasov's edifices embodied the idea of the feats of arms and the triumph of Russia in the war against Napoleon. The gates themselves and the chains of the railing are embellished with superimposed shields. This multi-column portico is in itself a type of architectural memorial recording the patriotic upsurge of the Russian people in defence of their motherland in 1812.

THE MOREA COLUMN

In the eastern part of the park, not far from the Hermitage, yet another monument commemorating a feat of arms, has been preserved. This is the Morea or Small Rostral Column, erected in 1771 to commemorate the victory of the Russian fleet at the peninsula of Morea in Greece.

Simple in its composition, the monument is a small seven-metre high column of greyish blue white veined Russian marble on a pedestal of the same stone. The column is topped by a small rostral obelisk of Italian pink marble. The monument bears an inscription glorifying the feat of the Russian seamen. "The Russian forces numbered six hundred men," it reads, "who did not ask how numerous the enemy was, but where he was; six thousand Turks were taken prisoner." The plaque also records that the impregnable fortress of Navarino surrendered to Brigadier Hannibal, the great grandfather of the poet, Alexander Pushkin.

The monuments commemorating feats of arms in Tsarskoye Selo are an inseparable part of the park and form an ensemble of exceptional artistic value. No wonder that one of Pushkin's contemporaries called Tsarskoye Selo "the Pantheon of Russian Glory".

THE LANDSCAPE PARK

The monuments commemorating feats of arms are located in the part of the Catherine Park laid out later on, the so-called Landscape Park occupying a vast territory to the south of the palace and easily visible from the southern terrace of the Cameron Gallery, which stands on the boundary between the two parts of the Catherine Park. From the terrace you get a view of the broad meadow with clumps of trees dotted about on it which descends the sloping hillside to the Great Pond, the compositional centre of the landscape park.

The creators of this type of park which had become the fashion in the 1770s were the architect Vasili Neyelov and the expert gardeners Johann Busch and Trifon Ilyin. Neyelov went to England where the new fashion had budded, to take a look at examples of landscape gardening, based on the principles of creating a garden like a piece of countryside untouched by man.

In landscape parks everything looks natural: big trees are planted haphazardly and numerously, providing shade even on hot days; there are winding, sometimes fanciful avenues and paths, ponds, and large clearings suddenly opening onto a fine view. Just as in a fairy-tale land, ruins, entwined in ivy, nestle amidst the luxuriantly overgrown trees, and old hump-back bridges span the canals. The park looks as if it has never been touched by human hand and nature has enhanced everything previously created here by man; even the statues seem to come to life, preserving the neglectedness of the secret woodland bower, the cosiness of the glades, the calm surfaces of the ponds with the silvery willows, tall maples, spreading limes and elms reflected in them. The well thought-out combinations of trees, bushes, and flowers, the interplay of thick groves, cascades of ponds and glades, marble bridges and decorative park pavilions, producing as it were, a mottled effect on the landscape background, are determined by the colours of the location, its topography and planning. The pavilions, little bridges, summer houses, columns, and the artificial mounds and hillocks blend well with the landscape.

In 1856, a considerable part of the landscape park was fenced off, and in 1865, the architect Andrei Vidov planned an intimate little court garden, the so-called "Private Garden". Its compositional centre was a large fountain with an octagonal pool and a tall vase of Carrara marble. Flower-beds, sculptures, paths, and trees were grouped symmetrically around the fountain.

The structures that have survived in the landscape park are distinguished by an amazing variety of architectural designs. Thus, for example, the pavilion the **Evening Hall** can easily be seen from the Private Garden and from the Kagul obelisk. It is built in restrained and laconic forms, with minimal ornamentation, except for a four-column

Granite terrace with sculpture of mythological figures.

A tower of the Egyptian Gates.

ditional name given to these structures. The building's composition and embellishments are unusual. The roof resting on twelve columns, with its fancifully curved edges and brightly painted figures of dragons at the corners, the figured outlines of the windows and doors, the open-work railing on the terrace and the fan-like staircase descending to the water, all reveal the architect's attraction to the picturesqueness and absorbing nature of Chinese park pavilions. This type of exotic architecture became widespread in Russia at the end of the 1760s.

THE CONCERT HALL

Of considerable interest among the surviving edifices of the landscape park there is a graceful pavilion designed by Giacomo Quarenghi, one of the most outstanding architects of the end of the eighteenth and the beginning of the nineteenth centuries.

Erected in the 1780s on an island formed by a network of canals, the hall was intended for concerts in summer. The façade of the single-storey pavilion overlooking the pond is embellished with a four-column portico and on the north-western side has a dome-capped rotonda. In the sole ornament on the smooth walls Quarenghi used a motif traditional in the architecture of ancient Rome: a moulded frieze in which garlands alternate with the heads of sacrificial bulls. Beyond the colonnade of the rotonda, there are five bas-reliefs of mythological content by the famous

Ionic portico and figures of caryatids between the window frames, enlivening its façade.

To the west of the Evening Hall on the boundary between the Catherine and the Alexander parks there stands an exotic-looking structure, the **Chinese** or **Creaking Summer House**.

It was built in 1778–1786 by the architect Yuri Felten. When they turn in the wind, the flag weather vanes attached to the roof of the summer house creak loudly, and this explains the tra-

eighteenth-century Russian sculptor Mikhail Kozlovsky. Solemn and laconic in style, they are a splendid addition to the austere architecture of the pavilion.

The interiors of the building are in the style of old classicism. The walls of the central hall finished with marble are embellished with pilasters of the Corinthian order, sculptured medallions, ornamental murals, and painted panels. The mosaic floor, the end of the second and beginning of the third century A.D., is particularly interesting. The mosaic depicts the myth about the abduction of Europa by Zeus.

The decor of the two chambers at the sides of the rotonda is permeated with the spirit of Antiquity. One of them is decorated with four bas-reliefs—allegories of painting, architecture, sculpture, and science; the second is adorned with painted panels depicting sacrifices.

At present, preparations are underway to restore this pavilion, which is a work of art of an eighteenth-century Russian park architecture.

Not far from the Concert Hall, in the middle of the main avenue in this part of the park, the Ramp Avenue, there rises the **Granite Terrace** designed by the architect Luigi Rusca at the beginning of the nineteenth century. Embellished with statues of mythological heroes, and an austere balustrade surrounded by parterres with flower-beds, the terrace is the most elegant spot in the park.

At the foot of the hill on which the Granite Terrace is located, among the tall trees there nestles one of the most lyrical sculptures in the park, "The Maiden with a Pitcher" or the "Milkmaid".

THE "MILKMAID" FOUNTAIN

The bronze statue of the maiden was created by the eminent Russian sculptor Pavel Sokolov in 1816. The subject of the fountain's composition is La Fontaine's fable "The Milkmaid" or the "Pitcher of Milk". The fable tells the story of a young milkmaid Peretta who daydreamed so much of being rich on her way to the market that she even jumped up in the air. The pitcher of milk that she was carrying broke and the milk was spilt. The saddened girl sat down by the broken pitcher at the side of the road. However, P. P. Sokolov imparted another meaning to the La Fontaine fable, which illustrated the transiency and illusory nature of human joys. An endless jet of water pours forth from the fragments of the broken pitcher, as if symbolising the eternity and inexhaustibility of life.

The girl's pose, touching in its helplessness, her gentle and exquisitely beautiful figure create a mood of serene and radiant sadness.

In August 1941, when preparing to evacuate the museum's treasures, the "Maiden with a Pitcher" was buried in the ground and therefore it did not suffer during the Nazi occupation.

INFORMATION

MUSEUMS

The Catherine Palace

Open from 10:00 to 17:00.
Closed on Tuesdays and the last Monday of every month.

The Agate Rooms

Open from 11:00 to 17:00 in the summer months only.
Closed on Tuesdays.

The Cameron Gallery

Permanent Exhibitions:
"Carriages, 17th-19th centuries".
Open daily in summer only from 11:00 to 17:00.
Closed on Thursdays.
"Costumes and decorative and applied art, 18th beginning of 20th centuries". The exhibition will give you an idea of the uniforms worn by the various types of troops in the Russian army in the 18th and 19th centuries, and of civilian clothes at the time. You will not only see uniforms, but also portraits of that time, weapons, orders, and regalia. So, each exhibit on display does, as it were, help to explain and supplement the other exhibits. Thus, next to a portrait of a young, beautiful maid of honour, dressed as was customary at court, there is a lady's toilet set, a fan, and a carved comb. This exhibition is frequently visited by film-makers, costume and stage designers, and book illustrators, all those who need to get an exact idea of 18th and 19th century Russian costumes for their work.

Open daily from 11:00 to 17:00.
Closed an Thursdays.